Walter D. Edmonds, Storyteller

LIONEL D. WYLD

D1713081

SYRACUSE UNIVERSITY PRESS

1982

This book is published with the assistance of a grant
from the John Ben Snow Foundation.

Parts of Chapters 4 and 6 dealing with Edmonds' novels *Rome Haul, Chad Hanna,*
and *The Boyds of Black River* were originally published in critical articles in *The
Midwest Quarterly, English Record,* and *English Journal* (National Council of Teachers of English).

Library of Congress Cataloging in Publication Data

Wyld, Lionel D.
    Walter D. Edmonds, storyteller.

    (A New York State Study)
    Bibliography: p.
    Includes index.
    1. Edmonds, Walter Dumaux, 1903–   . 2. Authors,
American—20th century—Biography. 3. New York (State)
in literature. I. Title.
PS3509.D564Z94 1982   813'.52 [B]   82-10443
ISBN 0-8156-0180-8

Manufactured in the United States of America

Walter D. Edmonds, Storyteller

A NEW YORK STATE STUDY

Walter D. Edmonds. Photograph by Sarah E. Broley, courtesy of Walter D. Edmonds.

For Janet and Kimberley

Lionel D. Wyld received the A.B. from Hamilton College and the A.M. and Ph.D. from the University of Pennsylvania. He is past president of the New York Folklore Society and of the American Studies Association of New York State and the author of *Low Bridge! Folklore and the Erie Canal.* He has taught literature, history, and American Studies at several universities, and his articles appear in leading professional and popular publications.

Contents

Preface

I FIRST MET WALTER D. EDMONDS on a Canal Society of New York State field trip on an August weekend. Earlier that year I had completed my doctoral studies at the University of Pennsylvania with a dissertation that included a section on Edmonds, appropriately titled, I felt, "Second Builder of the Grand Canal." The phrase was lifted from the citation read at a Union College commencement some years before when Edmonds was awarded an honorary degree. I had read most of Edmonds's books as well as everything I could find concerning the Erie Canal, and I had corresponded with the novelist in regard to my research into the history and folklore of canal times. That summer field trip took us over the route of the old Black River Canal, northward from Rome to Boonville. I took photographs of Mr. Edmonds talking with fellow canal buffs on a bridge overlooking the remains of the once proud canal and of "Northlands," the Edmonds farm outside Boonville, where he very kindly autographed my copy of *Rome Haul,* his first novel. My daughter Kimberley—at three, the youngest "canaller" on the field trip—and her mother patiently indulged their amateur photographer father and husband by posing for a picture or two in front of the white clapboard farmhouse. We had refreshments in that congenial North Country setting, and the occasion gave me an inkling of how this farm and the surrounding Black River Valley area could have inspired so much pleasurable literature.

Although I devoted a full chapter to Edmonds in my book, *Low Bridge! Folklore and the Erie Canal,* that study just teased an appetite already whetted by Edmonds's prodigious literary endeavors. Two study grants enabled me to track down and consult first hand the many magazine stories Edmonds had written, beginning with his publications at Harvard, and to compile a bibliography and checklist of his works. But, I thought, there just has to be a book about him. After all, Edmonds is a very talented short story writer and a historical novelist whose *Drums Along the Mohawk* (1936) has become a classic. An invitation to speak at a Syracuse University meeting of the College Conference on New York History gave me an opportunity to air some of my ideas on the multidisciplinary nature of regionalism; and my paper on "Folklore, Literature, and History" made use of a number of illustrations drawn from Edmonds's works. Along the way this book began taking shape.

Edmonds is a many-faceted author. The novels *Rome Haul* (1929) and *Erie Water* (1933), along with the regional stories like those collected in *Mostly Canallers* (1934), gave him a reputation as an interpreter of the times historians call "the Canal Era." He produced remarkably good short stories for more than a decade, publishing in such prominent periodicals as *Scribner's Magazine*, the *Atlantic Monthly*, the *Dial*, and the *Saturday Evening Post*, with many stories selected for reprinting in the annual *Best Short Stories* and *O. Henry Award* anthologies. With the publication of his Revolutionary War novel *Drums Along the Mohawk* in 1936, Edmonds achieved an established place in American literature as a historical novelist. The first of his many popular books for young readers, *The Matchlock Gun* (1941), won him the Newbery Medal of the American Library Association as the best book of the year, and his *Bert Breen's Barn* received the 1975 National Book Award for children's literature. *They Fought with What They Had* (1951), an account of the U.S. Air Force in the Pacific Theater in the Second World War, and *The Musket and the Cross* (1968), a study of the struggle of France and England for colonial North America that is one of Edmonds's own favorites among his works, showed that he could write history no less successfully than historical fiction.

Broadway and Hollywood both helped to bring Edmonds's name and novels before the general public. His first book, *Rome Haul*, became a Marc Connelly play on Broadway and resulted in two motion picture adaptations. Other novels—*Chad Hanna* (1940), a circus story set in central New York State in the early nineteenth century, and *Drums Along the Mohawk*, his Mohawk Valley tale of the colonials versus the British that was a Book-of-the-Month Club selection in 1936—followed suit in "going Hollywood."

These books, along with many similarly derived short stories, may well have inspired and influenced other authors to write about upstate New York. While *Rome Haul* is representative of a wide-ranging literature inspired by the epic building of New York State's Erie Canal, it is at the same time the forerunner of a plethora of adult and juvenile books dealing with the Erie experience. So much subsequent Erie-inspired fiction resulted from Edmonds's early work that Schenectady's Union College gave him that accolade as "the second builder of our Grand Canal." In literary terms, if one can call novels like Edmonds's *Rome Haul* and *Erie Water* a new or distinct genre, he deserves to be called the father of the canal novel. In the 1940s and 1950s especially, many such novels were published, as well as a rash of junior books that depicted the canal in story and picture.

Since the publication of *Rome Haul* in 1929, Walter D. Edmonds has been in the forefront of American regional writers. Yet Edmonds is never too narrowly regional, and his best work—like *Drums Along the Mohawk, Chad Hanna,* and *Rome Haul*—captures a sense of the epic of America. Perhaps, as Robert Frost once said of himself, Edmonds is in the best sense a synecdochist, whose regionalism actually evidences a national pride and the universal characteristics of people in every walk of life.

This book focuses upon Edmonds's fiction. It presents the circumstances of the author's early life and his background in upstate New York which helped to shape his writing, including the influence of his North Country boyhood, the Erie Canal, and his college years at Harvard. It traces his development as a short-story writer and novelist from his undergraduate days writing for the Harvard *Advocate* to his place in American letters as "senior short story writer" (as *Saturday Evening Post* editors called him) and historical novelist. It also analyses many of his short novels, the so-called books for young readers, and his overall contribution to children's literature.

To speak of Edmonds as a storyteller echoes a term he prefers to use himself in describing his work. Much if not most of that work has a sense of the oral tradition about it: a blending of fact, fiction, and folklore. He is squarely in line with an American storytelling tradition that stems from the days of the early pioneers' tales around the camp fire and includes the still-heard yarns of lumberjacks, miners, fishermen, and hunters today. For Edmonds it derives from his North Country environs, from the tales he heard from and about the upstate farm folk around Boonville, where he was born, and the canal boatmen plying the Black River and the Erie canals. The incorporation of folklore and folk life in his work is more than incidental, and his stories and novels are repositories for authentic and often mirthful Americana.

As a regional writer Edmonds is part, too, of a long tradition of New York State writers that includes James Fenimore Cooper, Philander Deming, Joseph Kirkland, Harold Frederic, Samuel Hopkins Adams, and Edward Noyes Westcott (whose *David Harum* became a minor classic in its delineation of the "Yorker" type). Edmonds also has roots in the folk tradition, in the exaggerations of Yorkers before him, like the Injun fighter Tom Quick or Leatherstocking (whether the "original" Nat Foster or Cooper's creation), in the comedy of frontier characters like Petroleum Vesuvius Nasby, the product of another upstate New Yorker, David Ross Locke, or the dry humor of David Harum, Westcott's homespun Syracusan.

Edmonds's novels and stories give evidence of his deep regard for American history. In re-creating the American past he writes with the knowledge gained through careful research. He uses history, but he looks beyond the usual, conventional data of history to learn of husking bees and hay mowing, how colonial women wove their stockings, and what settlers ate for supper, the price of a foamer of ale along the Kingsroad, how a canal lock worked, the argot of canallers and circus folk, and the colors their boats and wagons were painted. He is most of all the historian of people. His stories and novels focus upon the ordinary folk, basically independent in outlook and spirit, who comprise what Walt Whitman liked to call "aggregate America." They mind a farm, work a canal, play a calliope or a pianoforte, operate a sawmill, and, if necessary, fight a war. Edmonds's people—his characters—are human beings whom we meet in instances in their lives which demonstrate the common bonds that unite friend and foe, farmer and canaller, patriot and Tory, Indian and white, or Southerner and Yankee. He gives us no Odysseus, he creates no Hamlet, he writes of no Cyrano; yet throughout his work there runs the unmistakable Edmonds's stamp on characters who—in their ordinary lives of lights and darks, ups and downs, happinesses and despairs, adventures and misfortunes— have something of Odysseus in them, a little bit of Hamlet, a touch of Cyrano. This focus, as he has said, on the qualities of mind and spirit of ordinary people who carry the burden of human progress extends our vision of the present, our perception of history, and our meaning of heritage.

Cumberland, Rhode Island   Lionel D. Wyld
Spring 1982

Acknowledgment

To the man whose writing has so delighted me and whose cooperation and kindness in responding to an unpardonable number of questions are so deeply appreciated: WALTER D. EDMONDS.

Walter D. Edmonds, Storyteller

1

Background for a Writer

"TO BE ABLE TO DO FOR ONESELF in one's own way," wrote Walter D. Edmonds in his preface to *Two Logs Crossing* (1945), one of his books for young readers, "was the dream which first brought men to this land. There are a few people who confuse it with becoming rich, but money is not the American Dream and never has been. Money can be made of anything you choose, but a man's life is made of the courage, independence, decency, and self-respect he learns to use."[1]

Throughout his long writing career, whether in the novel, the short story, or the so-called books for young readers, Edmonds has held fast to this essential philosophy of rugged individualism. He writes historical fiction, but he prefers not to be known as a historical novelist. He has written critically acclaimed short stories, but he has never been one to challenge his contemporary fellow authors whose works are more apt to find a spot in the many college anthologies devoted to the genre. He has produced a significant number of books for young readers, garnering two national awards, although he used to say he never wrote a children's book.

Walter D. Edmonds says he is "a storyteller."[2] The term fits him. His writing draws not only upon the peculiarly personal experiences of his life and background but also upon the history of the country, the culture of his native state, and the folklore of his native region. In the latter sense, especially, Edmonds *is* a storyteller, drawing upon oral tradition and other elements of history and folk culture to incorporate into a literature that has earned him a firm reputation. Edmonds, in the words of the citation for an honorary Doctor of

1

Letters degree Harvard University awarded him, "is a teller of stories that delight a wide audience."

EDMONDS COUNTRY

Walter D. Edmonds was born in the Black River country of upstate New York, a region that is particularly rich in native lore. In earlier times the Oneida and the Onondaga Indians roamed throughout the territory, which has long been known for extremes of climate that produce rugged and hardy individualists.

The Black River itself is nature's maverick, flowing generally from east to west; it drains nearly two thousand square miles in the North Country through which it flows. The source of the river lies in what is now Herkimer County and a part of the Adirondack State Forest Preserve. It carries its waters from these Adirondack origins some 115 miles north and west, while the state's more widely known St. Lawrence and Mohawk rivers follow an eastward course. Much of the Black River consists of cascades and rapids, with "Great Falls" (Watertown) and "High Falls" (Lyons Falls) tumbling water which at one time powered mills and aided the early development of industry. It is a region of veritable contrasts, suitably inspiring for a writer-to-be in its variety, from its subzero, snow-filled winters to blossom-fragrant spring days and golden splashes of color in the autumn.

"The North Country has a cleanliness about it," wrote Howard Thomas in describing the region. "Smog and pollution are absent. Crisp breezes off Lake Ontario may make trees around Copenhagen lean as they grow, but they put roses in the cheeks of North Country girls. Over the years since the first New Englanders fought their way through the wilderness, inhabitants of the North Country have become reconciled to the capriciousness of the Black River and to the rigors of winters which make them probably the healthiest people in the State."[3]

The more immediate inspiration for what were later to become stories and novels of New York State "canawlers" was the Black River Canal. Suggested by Governor DeWitt Clinton as early as 1825, the canal was begun in 1838 and completed in 1855. Like its larger and more famous predecessor, the Erie Canal, it proved to be an engineering marvel and a maker of history in its own right. For one thing, the Black River Canal had more locks than any other canal in the world, as many as seventy of them in one segment between Boonville, where the Edmondses had their farm, and the Erie Canal at Rome. This Black River Canal, with its many locks and hardy boaters, was to serve Edmonds particularly often as the setting and the source of characters for his fiction. Lumbering, boatbuilding, hauling, and other industries thrived in that region in the latter part of the nineteenth century as a result of the canal. The canal became an artery of commerce for North Country towns and villages, providing even small hamlets with connections to the larger commercial centers of Syracuse, Buffalo, and Albany.

The influence upon Edmonds of this upstate New York background is large. "When a boy gets raised in the Black River Valley of New York State's North Country," wrote fellow New York author Carl Carmer, "he has learned a lot by the time he is ready to go away to school."[4] Growing up in Boonville gave Edmonds a healthy, nature-centered boyhood, one in which nature in general and farm life in particular occupied his time. And there were always the boaters of the canal. "When I was small," he said in an autobiographical note, "boats still inched along the Black River Canal, across the valley from our farm . . . and provided a mysterious backdrop of a different life to my own, which was entirely absorbed in the operations of the large dairy and general farm maintained by my father."[5] Even as he grew older, Boonville and the farm always beckoned, and until the publication of his first novel at the age of twenty-five, Edmonds spent all but one summer on the farm. It was there he came to know the people who later formed the basis for characters in many of his stories and novels. From fishing and canoeing in the Black River Canal and from watching the canal boats go by, loaded with sand, potatoes, lumber, and other freight, he was later to derive the inspiration for the themes of much of his fiction.[6]

The Boonville into which Walter Dumaux Edmonds, Jr., was born on July 15, 1903, had a population of some two thousand persons. They were dairymen mostly, with a sprinkling of lumbermen, mechanics, cheese-makers, and others typical of an upstate farm and canal community of the early 1900s. His father, Walter D. Edmonds, Sr., who maintained a patent law practice in New York City, had inherited the thousand-acre family home, "Northlands," through Walter's grandfather, John Henry Edmonds, known by the courtesy title of "Judge" Edmonds. His grandfather, who originally lived in Utica,

The "Northlands" farmhouse, the Edmonds place near Boonville, where the historical novelist and short story writer was born. The farm and the surrounding Black River Valley area provided Edmonds with themes and characters for many stories and sketches. Photograph courtesy of Walter D. Edmonds and the photographer, Benjamin A. Fairbank.

New York, acquired considerable farm property including "Northlands" when he sold his holdings in the Utica-Schenectady Telegraph Company. "I'm told that if he held on to that stock," Walter has reflected wryly, "today it would be worth millions."[7] The Utica-Schenectady Telegraph is one of the five companies that merged to form Western Union.

Many persons who have sought out Edmonds at the farm will attest to the fact that "Northlands" is not easy to find. It has a Boonville address, but the farm lies south of the village off Hawkinsville Road (Route 12B). A visit to the author at the farm in 1974 by Edmund Wilson's biographer Richard Costa is typical:

> The tipoff to Walter D. Edmonds' "Northlands" is a large red rural mailbox. At that point one turns left, past a sign that urges *drive slowly, children.* The main house—for there is a complex of houses—is clapboarded and rambling. A driveway leads to a fence, beyond which there appear to be cornfields. I park and walk to the front door. "I'm Kay Edmonds," says a trimly attractive woman at the door. . . . Kay Edmonds says she will summon her husband. He appears, a tall, slender man in logger's jacket and work trousers. A stocky terrier . . . keeps vying for my attention, and I am glad to give it. "It's a Jack Russell terrier," Edmonds reports after introductions. "Name's Erlo, which I thought was original but isn't. Comes from something in upstate lore."
>
> I follow as Edmonds walks up two steps to what proves to be his study. I ask him to account for "that wonderful sound," and he beckons me to the window. I walk to a far window beyond his writing desk and look out on a brook where water flows over rocks. "We've had trout out there all summer."[8]

"I believe I shall always think of that view from his writing table as what writers talk about," Costa concluded, "when they talk about the ideal atmosphere." Certainly the farm was a never-ending source of story material for Edmonds, from the first sketch, on hunting snowshoe rabbits, he sold to *Forest and Stream* in 1924 to his more recent stories like that of the field mice in *Time To Go House* (1969) who move into the farmhouse in winter.

Edmonds used to summer regularly at the farm, but he now lives year round in Concord, Massachusetts. He sold "Northlands" in December 1976, and, he says, he has not been back to see the place, "which has been lumbered by the new owners down to four inches on the stump. It was a lovely place, from my point of view anyhow," he confided, adding, "sometimes I miss it, but this house and garden [in Concord], going down to the Sudbury River, have compensations."[9]

His middle name, Dumaux, came to Walter through his paternal French grandmother, Eugenie Dumaux, daughter of Jean Dumaux and Marie Ducroix; but Walter, who tried unsuccessfully to drop the name, finally compromised with family sentiment by re-

Another view of "Northlands," which was the Edmonds summer home until he sold the farm in 1976. Photograph courtesy of Walter D. Edmonds and the photographer, Benjamin A. Fairbank.

taining the initial. His mother descended from the Mays. One of them, Edmonds said, "assisted at the Salem witch business,"[10] but he publicly repented afterward. Later the Mays were more liberal in their community stance. His great-grandfather on the May side, a Unitarian minister, used his Syracuse, New York, house as a station on the Underground Railroad of Civil War times; and he counted among his friends and acquaintances such notable Abolitionists as Gerritt Smith and William Lloyd Garrison. Edmonds briefly introduced "a Reverend Mr. May from Syracuse" in one of his early novels; this liberal minister runs a branch of the Underground Railroad, and he preaches sermons about "Universal Brotherhood."[11] On Judge Edmonds's side of the family the ancestry is traceable to

Peter Bulkeley, the first minister in Concord, Massachusetts, where the Edmondses reside. The family names survive in Edmonds's three children, his son Peter Bulkeley Edmonds, and two daughters, Eleanor Dumaux and Sarah May Edmonds.

EDUCATION

Prior to attending Harvard, Walter completed his secondary education, after attending the Cutler Day School in New York City and St. Paul's School in Concord, New Hampshire, at the Choate School in Wallingford, Connecticut. "To me, however," Edmonds reflected many years later, "the winters were a mere filling of time; and the life on the farm filled practically all my imagination."[12] The only affiliation perhaps worthy of special note to his literary development during these years is his membership on the board of the *Choate Literary Magazine,* which was an elective honor. Edmonds was considered an excellent student with considerable academic potential, as is indicated by reports sent from the Choate School to his parents. "Another splendid report for Walter!" said one of these reports. "He is first or second in every class of which he is a member." "And we like Walter as much out of his class work as we admire and respect him in it!" read another. "He fits into every department of his school life with full energy and friendly cooperation."[13]

But despite such comments by his teachers, which indicate their high regard for the young Edmonds both as a pupil and as a person, he looked upon the preparatory school days with disinterest at best. Later, when he took up his studies at Harvard, he admitted that "for the first time in my life, I began to enjoy school."[14]

Harvard signified more than adapting to study; it marked the beginning of Edmonds's literary career. During the first year at Cambridge he became an editor of the *Harvard Advocate,* the undergraduate literary publication, and he contributed an impressive number of stories and other pieces while he was still an underclassman. His father wanted Walter to become a chemical engineer; but having squeaked by chemistry with a "C," he made up his mind that science was not for him and decided to concentrate in English. When an upperclassman he served the *Advocate* as its secretary and president; and his literary contributions—short stories, a few poems, and several reviews—continued to keep pace. All told, within a year after his graduation, by 1927, Edmonds had completed about twenty short stories, including, in addition to many pieces of fiction published in the *Advocate* between 1922 and 1926, stories sold to *Scribner's Magazine*, the *Dial*, and the *Atlantic Monthly*.

"Walter was a shy youngster," wrote his good friend and fellow author David McCord, when he reflected afterward upon Edmonds's Harvard days. "His circle of college friends," said McCord, "seemed small but sympathetic. He said very little to strangers; and even ripening acquaintance did not carry one rapidly to the hidden oracle."[15] The real influence at Harvard on Edmonds, however, was neither the *Advocate* nor any student associations. As a junior he enrolled in English 12, a by then long-famous advanced composition course taught by one of Harvard's greats: Professor Charles Townsend Copeland, known affectionately as "Old Copey" to countless Harvard men.

Through Professor Copeland's classes a veritable stream of literary talent has passed—T. S. Eliot, Robert Benchley, Stanley Kunitz, Bernard DeVoto, Brooks Atkinson, Frederick Lewis Allen, Conrad Aiken, and Oliver LaFarge, to name just a few. Not all of these Harvard alumni recall Professor Copeland's old-fashioned methods and his caustic wit to their liking, but most of his students frankly acknowledged the extent of his influence in producing writers. Donald J. Adams, in his biography of Old Copey, called Edmonds a student in whose accomplishments Professor Copeland took great pride,[16] and Edmonds's name and that of Robert E. Sherwood, another of Copey's last students to achieve literary fame, are closely linked in the years after Harvard.

Professor Copeland saw in Walter the storyteller's instinct for detail and authentic color, and he respected the young man's industry. Edmonds was a hard worker, a quality of temperament which later proved valuable in disciplining himself, following his graduation, when he sat down purposefully to write short stories and then a novel. The respect between Edmonds and his mentor was mutual. "If Copey had lived in the days of Elisha," said Edmonds, "he would have been set down in the Bible as a prophet."[17] Copeland's careful concern for language and his interest in reading aloud especially appealed to the student and the fledgling writer. He later recalled these characteristics as praiseworthy attributes. "I have always had a clearer consciousness of the writer, from hearing Copey read a page from his work," he told his fellow author when J. Donald

Adams was compiling material for his biography of the educator, "than a year's course with any other man."[18]

The Harvard years were fruitful for Edmonds. He graduated with the class of 1926, missing out on honors in English because he had failed to satisfy a requirement in Anglo-Saxon for George Lyman Kittredge, a professor later to garner his widest reputation as a Shakespearean text editor and scholar. With appropriate irony, Edmonds and Professor Kittredge were drawn together at another commencement when, a decade later, both received honorary degrees for their achievements from Union College in Schenectady, New York.

Recognition for Edmonds has generally kept pace with his pen. Beginning with the praises of Professor Copeland during his student days at Harvard, it has come to him from several routes: the frequent inclusion of his work, especially during the 1930s, in the popular and annual short story anthologies; the acceptance by the public of a number of his novels and their Hollywood adaptations; the awards to his children's books; and the honorary degrees offered by some of the better known colleges and universities in the East. The first of these, appropriately enough for the Boonville author, came to Edmonds from a venerable college in upstate New York. In awarding him a Litt.D. degree, President Dixon Ryan Fox of Union College called Edmonds "the second builder of our Grand Canal," pridefully focusing special attention on his novels and short stories dealing with the region's historic Erie Canal. The year was 1936, the same year in which Edmonds's best-selling work, *Drums Along the Mohawk,* came out. Other honorary degrees for the writer followed: awards from Rutgers University in 1940, from Colgate University in 1947, and from his alma mater, Harvard University, in 1952.

Before taking a closer look at some of the short stories and the major novels which have helped to make this reputation, it seems appropriate to examine first the influence of Edmonds's college education and, especially, the prodigious number of pieces the young author had published in the *Advocate* during the years he was a student at Harvard College.

2

Apprenticeship at Harvard

*E*DMONDS'S AFFILIATION WITH THE *HARVARD ADVOCATE* extended through practically all his undergraduate days at Cambridge. During this period his published effort for the undergraduate monthly included more than a dozen and a half short stories, in addition to occasional articles, editorial commentary, reviews of books, and poetry. As a result of his numerous contributions, it is little wonder that he later admitted feeling that he had spent more time and effort on the *Advocate* than on his curricular studies.[1] But the advantage of such writing and of the affiliation to a person of literary bent is undeniable: Edmonds's interest in the *Advocate* and his work on its editorial staff placed him in contact with numerous other students whose literary talents were to become well recognized in the years to follow.[2]

Among these figures were Dudley Fitts, class of 1925, poet and classicist who went on to teach at Phillips Andover Academy; John Finley, another member of the class of '25, who preceded Edmonds as president of the *Advocate* and was later named Eliot Professor of Greek at his alma mater and served as a collaborator on the famed Harvard University report, *General Education in a Free Society;* Oliver La Farge, another president of the *Advocate,* who wrote the novel *Laughing Boy* which won the Pulitzer Prize in 1929; and poet James Gould Cozzens, who was a member of Edmonds's class. During these years Professor Copeland, Edmonds's respected teacher in English 12, along with poet Witter Bynner, Harvard '12, served on the faculty advisory board to the magazine.

Edmonds's connection with the Cambridge periodical included regular advancements on the magazine's editorial staff, culminating in his being named president of the *Advocate* in his senior year at Harvard. His name appeared first—it was signed "Walter D. Edmonds, Jr." then, and for all his later *Advocate* stories—on the list of associate editors for the issue of June 1922. Edmonds became secretary of the *Advocate* during the tenure of John Finley as president; the announcement came in the same issue (March 1924) which carried an Edmonds short story, "Up-River Mists and Lilacs," that won the P. W. Thayer Prize for "the most notable piece of writing published in the *Advocate* during 1924." With the issue of February 1925, Edmonds became president-elect of the monthly, and the full announcement read: "The following officers have been elected for the ensuing year: *President,* Walter D. Edmonds, Jr., '26; *Secretary,* Charles Allen Stuart, '26; *Treasurer,* Winthrop Wetherbee, Jr., '26; *Pegasus,* Richard Edsall, '26; *Business Manager,* Samuel Whiting, '26."

While president, Edmonds added to an already impressive list of short story contributions to the *Advocate* his reviews of James Boyd's *Drums* and of other current fiction, two poems, and campus commentary and other essays. In the spring of 1925, he was partner as president-elect to one of the more successful parody issues of the magazine. This classic number went by another name—it was the *Advocate*'s April issue, which was published as *The Dial;* it featured among its many notable pieces such parodies as "Anna's Ham," by Oneway Waistcoat (Glenway Westcott); "Halitosis," by Marianne Most (Marianne Moore); "Three Poems," by O. O. Goings (e. e. cummings); and "Wincklemann Among the Teacups," by T. S. Tellalot (T. S. Eliot).

Thus it was at Harvard College—and notably as a result of the *Advocate* experience—that Walter Dumaux Edmonds's future career as an author was fashioned. Since he published continuously in the *Advocate* in those years from 1922 to 1926, his work there bears scrutiny as a means of understanding the development of Edmonds as a maturing writer.

THE *ADVOCATE* SHORT STORIES

"'Jehu'" was the first short story by Edmonds to appear in the *Harvard Advocate:* it came in the 1921 Christmas number (dated January 1922). Edmonds's name was auspiciously carried on the magazine cover, along with Oliver La Farge's. "'Jehu'" was a good beginning. Set in upstate New York, it is a regional anecdote with a touch of humor and a touch of irony. The story, covering five *Advocate* pages, drew upon the college author's North Country background, for it deals with an episode in the life of Chippy Billenbeck, "universally acclaimed as the best fisherman in the county," who wins a race with a horse "trained back'ards."

During the remainder of Edmonds's first academic year, two more of his short stories appeared in the magazine. In the March issue "The Last of the Black Dwarfs" introduced the Coldenstaney gypsy twins from the Erie Canal fens. This story of blackguards and scoundrels is often amateurish in its dialogue and blatantly melodramatic, but it is important to the student of literary beginnings. The story, says Edmonds, was "a kind of fantastic development from Dickensian scenes of the marshes in *Great Expectations* combined with the Black River Canal."[3]

"Black Maria," which appeared in the *Advocate*'s May 1922 issue, is a considerably better story. "Black Maria" took Honorable Mention in the *Advocate* Short Story Contest that year. The story was selected, many years later, to represent Edmonds's *Advocate* fiction in Donald Hall's *Harvard Advocate Anthology* (1950). It was a good choice for, while it does not deal with the regional upstate New York characters frequently found in Edmonds's later work, the ingredients add up to a typical Edmonds story. The very colloquial opening, "'Huh,' said the skipper"; the description of the skipper's "ancient dory, painted brightly green, with its cargo of nasturtiums"; and the depiction of the snug sitting room in which the old skipper, Plunket, sat with his angular, bony wife—all these bear the Edmonds stamp.

This tale—along with his first two upstate New York stories —served notice that Edmonds could handle the colloquial, even slangy speech of a seaman or fisherman and arrest a reader's attention with devices that add a folklore atmosphere that he so often achieves in his later writing. As Black Maria is gradually revealed, in this tale-within-a-tale, the reader shares with the narrator the sobering bewilderment that the famed creature about whom so many exotic and adventurous stories had arisen was a hen!

> "Can this," I exclaimed, "can this be Black Maria?"
> "As ever was," the skipper assured me.

"But I thought she saved your life in mid-ocean; that she made you what you are, the best sailing master on the coast, before you retired."

"Gospel—every word," said the skipper.

How Black Maria saved Plunket's life against the combined saber-rattling of two opposing and very threatening gunboat admirals succeeds in a fashion that indicates the author's developing literary kinship with the frontier humorists of the nineteenth century. And, finally, there is the curious mixture of absurd and down-to-earth acceptance of the conditions of human living. The former skipper's wife managed to get rid of her rival by feeding it "Lay-or-Bust," and Plunket's reflection of his "fine figger of a he . . . " gets checked in time: "'It don't apply,' he mourned; then, catching a glimpse of Mrs. Plunket's bones, he went on, happily, 'A fine figger of a woman, sir, ain't she?'"

The issues of the *Advocate* for the 1922–23 academic year carried two of Edmonds's stories: "The Old 'Uns," a story about an old, frontier type doctor, and "The Blood of His Father," which has an unlocalized island setting. "Blue Eyes," a shipboard tale of greed and pearls, appeared in a fall issue. The January 1924 issue contained his "Saint Bon and the Organist of Midnight Mass," which won him his first P. W. Thayer Prize, and his first published poem, a nine-line romantic lyric called "Tonight." Edmonds's stories also appeared in the *Advocate* in the February, March, and June issues of that year. Two of them were closely linked to his developing emphasis on humanistic themes in essentially regional or local color settings.

The March issue carried "Up-River Mists and Lilacs," his second Thayer Prize story. Edmonds presents one of his most familiar character types in this short story, precursive of the heroes of later stories like "Tom Whipple, The Acorn, and the Emperor of Russia" (see Chapter 3) and the novels *Chad Hanna* and *Young Ames* (discussed in Chapter 6): the young lad who gazes out at the world, as it were, and will make it his. A philosophic current runs through this *Advocate* story, however, that goes deeper into the psychology of such archetypal quests. A momentary holding back occurs when the youth, John, meets his father, who has returned after long wandering, like the Eugene O'Neill figure in *Beyond the Horizon* which the story brings to mind. In response to the boy's inquiries about the cities "outside," his father protests that the cities and the wandering "ain't the half"—"It's the woods and the sky and the sea." "It ain't the wandering that counts," he tells the boy,"that ain't the half, son; it's the coming back home."

But youth does not listen to age. The lad thinks of the hills and of home, but he strikes off on the road to Yost's, the canal boater who is getting ready to leave for Rome, the junction of the Black River Canal and the Erie. Rome is the touch with civilization beyond the homeland hills; and this story foreshadows the opening of *Rome Haul,* the novel Edmonds was to write in the first years after Harvard. The boy John in "Up-River Mists and Lilacs" could easily be the literary ancestor of that novel's Dan Harrow, who left the Black River hills to find maturity on the bustling Erie Canal.

In "The Hills" (June 1924) Edmonds again drew heavily upon his upstate background, as he wrote another story which contains much of his personal philosophy of life and of writing. It is a story of maturity, or rather, maturing, like so many of his stories and even novels that were written later, and of boys-become-men that were yet to be created, who have names like Dan Harrow, Chad Hanna, John Ames, and Jerry Fowler. The story is, however, one of the eternal contrasts not only between boy and man, but between city and country; for the boy leaves his birthplace "deep in the highest hills" to follow his yearnings into manhood, dreaming his dreams of building upon his certain "prophecy of achievement" amid urban settings. Edmonds had written, in "The Hills" an allegory of life, one that is particularized in the North Country youth Loring, who ultimately finds—as his inner dream of youth fades into the past to become the disillusioned realism of age—that perspective is obtainable finally, and only, in the regions where he was born; in the hills there is an eternal wisdom and an eternal message.

Loring had the feeling of the unvanquished and the unconquerable, as he became a self-made man among men:

> The years rolled by and all that he wished for became his, but still he could look upon his possessions and say, "All this is mine, because I have made it for myself." He had become utterly a creature of the world and its thirst for vain accomplishment. Like the others, he hailed each petty step forward as a triumph of science and the wisdom of the human mind. He took up books, dashed off by famous writers in the heat of their progress, and he read them as they were written, pronouncing them, as did their authors, to be universal and pregnant with immortality. The long periods of ur-

gency brought silver into his hair, but he worked on and on, until his fame spread beyond the farthest bounds of his own country and flew abroad. Foreign nations called to him and he went among them and made them as he had of his people. The marks of his brain stood as monuments athwart the world, over the rivers, on the deserts, in the forests, on the plains, atop the mountains, and beneath the sea. And when he had carried his greatness into all parts of the earth, he lifted his eyes to the sky and said, "As I dreamed, I have done; as I have prophesied, I have accomplished; my name is among men, and I am great."

But like the narrator of Walt Whitman's poem who encounters the Learn'd Astronomer, Loring unaccountably became restless, less sure of his once eagerly sought fame; he became aware also that the city and the technology which he had once reached for in his youthful dreams of achievement and material success did not hold the answers. As Loring beheld the stars and "gazed into the darkness where the constellations wheeled in their slow procession, the realization came to him that wisdom was not his."

When, as on a pilgrimage, he returned to the hills of his birth, he encountered an old man, like a prophet out of Zion, who brought him back to the eternal realities. "You went down among men," said the stranger to Loring, "and you did great things, . . . but you saw the sky clear in the end, and you knew it was nothing you'd done but go in a circle, like the man who is lost in the dark without the stars. Bridges and buildings will crumble and fall, and the men underneath them will weary and die; but the hills must live forever, and the streams flow; and will the men and the beasts grow tired?"

Edmonds describes the old man as a seer, and his philosophy of the hills gives Loring the perspective he had never found in his search for fame, position, and material success. The hills become, in Edmonds's allegory, the symbol of stability, of permanence in the flux of life. "Everything's in the hills," the seer says, "I have learned to hear them and to see them; some day, I may even touch them; for the hills give—but they never take away."

In the following fall issues of the *Advocate*, September and November 1924, two more of Edmonds's stories were published. One, "The Coming of Jan," is a canal region story, the other an unlocalized tale about an organ grinder. These were followed in January by one of the most oft-cited of Edmonds's early works, "The Hanging of Kruscome Shanks."

Charles Grayson, in selecting this tale for inclusion in his anthology, *Stories for Men*, wrote that "'The Hanging of Kruscome Shanks' offers material to the student of literary beginnings."

> . . . That an undergraduate might write so well may not surprise those who recall that Scott Fitzgerald wrote "Tarquin of Cheapside" while at Princeton, John Dos Passos did "The Garbage Man" for the Harvard Dramatic Society, and Thornton Wilder, "The Angel That Troubled the Waters" for that of Yale, while grand old Doc Blanchard knew Sidney Howard had it from the day the long boy turned in "The Hollyhock Lad" as an English theme at California. But it is significant to note how Edmonds' preoccupation with the canal country dates back.[4]

The story does have much "canal" in it—the boats, the dank marsh, the fog, the bullfrogs, the reeds, the towpath, the mules, the men. But the story is not about the canal; it is about two highwaymen who help Kruscome Shanks escape a state execution by shooting him as he stands upon the gallows. The highwaymen, Jo Calash and Solomon Tinkle, reappear later in Edmonds's work, as do the atmosphere and the setting. This story helped give Edmonds recognition beyond the Cambridge campus when Henry T. Schnittkind and Horace C. Baker chose it to represent Harvard writing in their annual anthology of *The Best Short Stories 1924–25*.

Other canal stories appeared in the *Advocate* during Edmonds's final year at Harvard. Especially notable are "The Death of Jotham Klore" (September 1925), a short story in which he introduced a character who would figure prominently as the bully of the Erie Canal in his first novel, *Rome Haul*, in 1929, and "Solomon Tinkle's Christmas Eve," in which one of the renegades who figured in the story of Kruscome Shanks reappears in a gruff but sentimental tale. In addition to the Solomon Tinkle story, the December 1925 number of the magazine carried another tale, "The Three Wise Men," written by Edmonds under the pseudonym of Jean Dumaux. His last story for the *Advocate*, unlike his first one in the periodical, was neither regional nor particularly characteristic; it was "The North Turret Chamber" (February 1926), and with it Walter Edmonds closed the book on his Harvard apprenticeship. The *Advocate* had published more than twenty of his stories, certainly an impressive record of accepted contributions even for an undergraduate magazine.

OTHER CONTRIBUTIONS TO THE *ADVOCATE*

While short fiction forms the bulk of Edmonds's contributions to the *Advocate* during his college years, the genre was by no means his exclusive concern. Indeed, during his senior year at Harvard his writing was especially varied and included poems, book reviews and articles, as well as the several short stories. In one article he suggested "that Harvard give two degrees—the social, and the academic"[5]; in another he discussed the natural world of a Boonville Isaac Walton in an essay on "The Platonic Fisherman." In the issue for September 1925 he reviewed James Boyd's *Drums*, published that year—a work so obviously close to the reviewer's own developing regionalism that his comments bear examining.

Edmonds's style in the review, no less than his comments, reveals his developing sense of language—his mastery of the rhetorical power that Professor Copeland showed him was there to be refined into a honed tool of the storyteller. "As a narrative of the Revolution," the young reviewer said, "*Drums* is of little value; as a picture of the times, *Drums* is a most vivid piece of work; as a presentation of pre-Revolution atmosphere, restless and hesitant, yet determined, *Drums* is overwhelming in its completeness." He found the effect of the title symbol throughout: "The muttering of the drums is felt at the beginning. The gathering crescendo is irresistible; its final dying to silence thrilling. . . ." As for the content and narrative method of *Drums*, Edmonds criticized the lack of continuity and considered it "the sole weakness of the book. Though in themselves the scenes are excellent and often stirring, they have little sustained strength." This final summation about Boyd's novel seems, in retrospect, almost ironic; for later critics were to level similar charges against Edmonds's own Revolutionary War novel, *Drums Along the Mohawk*. However, Edmonds learned by the mid-1930s to avoid James Boyd's error of discontinuity.

One other review by Edmonds, of Sheila Kaye-Smith's *Starbrace*, a 1926 book, comes closer to providing a clue to Edmonds's early philosophy of writing fiction. "Though compelling the reader to sympathize with her characters," he wrote in the May 1926 *Advocate,* "she never allows them to sentimentalize. She is too sound and too honest, . . . her sense of tragedy, though sharp, is never admitted; not once are her nerves unstrung." "One feels," Edmonds wrote, touching upon an area he himself could well appreciate, "that she had the feel of soil upon her hands." The style of *Starbrace*, he noted, was "too well formed to permit brilliance, the author's sense of proportion too acute to let her seek verbal cleverness for its own sake."

Earlier in that final Harvard year he had reviewed for the October issue a new novel by Leslie Reid, one dealing with a cleric whom God never quite pardoned for his sinning but who, so went the legend, was to find God through one of his successors.[6] The book itself may not be important, but its theme is related to Edmonds's next venture into poetry, "The Abbot Speaks," which appeared in the following month's *Advocate*. As the abbot narrator of Edmonds's poem lies dying, his confessional is a simple telling of his life's need to his ministerial replacement:

> . . . Don't start, brother—don't let what
> I say disturb the pompous platitude
> Of prayer to fit the kicking of my heels
> Which these smug, snivelling idiots have taught
> You. You are one of this damned, holy brood;
> But I'm your fat old abbot saying what he feels.
> You're young to be an abbot, though a score
> Of years have passed since you first came
> To swell the holiness of this old abbey's fame.
> You seem to feel religion's beauty more
> Than I did when I passed the outer door
> To steal a small salvation for my name.
> And you will be an abbot without blame;
> Where I, your predecessor, kept a whore.
> Oh yes!—When I had washed away my fear
> With fasting, the desire in me grew
> To leave a seed of my new sanctity,
> A planted thistle, growing rankly here,
> Beside this smug, old gate-post.—No one knew:
> The others prayed too busily to see.
> Don't damn me, brother, with your hardened creed
> Too suddenly.

The poem bespeaks an understanding humanism that seems at the core of much of Edmonds's work, in the novel as well as in his shorter fiction. The strivings of individuals against convention, routine, dogma, drabness—against whatever it is that would suppress rather than uplift the human spirit—Edmonds captures with superb

understatement. Echoes of Robert Browning and Robert Frost are
found in the closing lines of the poem:

> If you had seen her, you would understand:
> She was small-lipped, and white. Her breasts
> Were soft. On her left arm there was a mole
> I used to kiss,—don't interrupt,—each brow
> Joined each, a quiet arch . . . My son, it rests
> With you. Long praying's needed for my soul.
> . . . If she were here, I'd do it over now . . .

Appropriately enough, this poem was also included (along
with the short story mentioned earlier) to represent Edmonds's writing in 1950 in the *Harvard Advocate Anthology*. But in all, only
three poems by Edmonds appeared in the *Advocate;* the young
writer obviously found prose a more congenial and fruitful genre.

THE HARVARD YEARS: EVALUATION

Edmonds's college literary output, particularly the characteristics
revealed in his fiction, reflected a keen interest in regionalism; and it
showed him, also, to be typically the beginning writer experimenting
with various modes, techniques, and subjects. His *Harvard Advocate* stories cannot be neatly categorized. Not surprisingly, a good
many of them deal with the canal area of upstate New York or with
other aspects of the North Country region with which he was familiar as a boy. Others, like the first Thayer Prize story, "Saint Bon and
the Organist of Midnight Mass," indicate that his interests were not
confined to exclusively regional themes; in this *Advocate* award
story and others he evidences a deep concern for individual human
beings regardless of time or place. A few stories, written in semi-
gothic style and full of romantic style imaginings, are reminiscent of
Edgar Allan Poe and other writers of the romantic age.

Some of Edmonds's early stories are period pieces, made up
of what are perhaps appropriately described as historical costume
episodes. Most of these, interestingly enough, have to do in some
way or other with the sea. "The Blood of His Father" (February

1923), with its island setting, deals with a boy of twelve left to the care of a madame; the greed-aboard-ship theme of "Blue Eyes" (November 1923) is a tale of avarice whose psychological gothic content is suggestive of Robert Louis Stevenson's story "Markheim"; "Julie" (February 1924) offers the reader a not-so-naive girl who acts out her role of maiden-in-distress in the vicinity of Mere d'Eau, Haiti; and the "The Devil's Angels" (February 1925) tells of a slave trader whose ship went down on the rip off Nantucket Island in 1748, and of the macabre happenings fourteen years later when the captain's sons come to grips with a witch's prophecy. And Edmonds's final submission to the *Advocate,* "The North Turret Chamber" (February 1926) especially brings Poe to mind. It has literary kinship with "The Haunted Palace" and with the fateful occurrences in the Usher story; Edmonds's Hohenhausen tale ends with the sombre note that "the only sound in the castle hall was the rush of rain upon the high roof, like echoing laughter."

In the majority of the short stories, regardless of their setting in place or time, Edmonds's underlying concern for man is unmistakable. It is often tinged with pathos and irony, like the human condition itself. Thus in "The Old 'Uns" (November 1922) Old Doc Hartlett and his horse Jasper ford the flooded Calamity Creek on a mission of mercy which a new and younger doctor would not accept, and at the end of the story both man and horse—the old 'uns—are dead, but not until after their mission is accomplished. In "The Death of Jotham Klore" (September 1925) we find a blind priest called to administer the last rites to the very man whose brutality caused the cleric's blindness; in "The Second Knave" (October 1925), an old card player finally realizes his lifelong ambition to have a double pinochle, though he dies from the shock of his victory; and in "Solomon Tinkle's Christmas Eve" (December 1925), two highwaymen, as bad as they come, show an uncommonly honest concern for the romantic, fragile notions of a naive young barmaid.

In each of these short stories the people are real, and the situation is regionally authentic. We realize in these undergraduate stories that Edmonds's interests center on the heroism of ordinary people and that his principal talent lies in the delineation of the folk. This characteristic is to carry over into his longer fiction, from novels about canallers to his *Drums Along the Mohawk.* His heroes and plots are never created in bold outlines: there is no epical heroism or blatant display of either strength or emotion. The heroic in an Edmonds story is more often than not a personal victory of an unsensational sort, or one which has its significance only in the folk context and the immediate, usually narrow, locale.

In these early stories written at Harvard his effectiveness in ably handling description is already apparent. He is sensitive to the nuances of life and of nature. He can, for instance, aptly create the atmosphere of a boy at the coming of spring: "All about him he heard the sound of the spring. The water was running underneath the snow down the hill before him. It trickled away in drops and ticked as it worked through the sand. On the hills, the deep blue shadows of winter had turned to vermillion and purple and a mass of dark clouds were climbing the southern sky. The sun was drinking the mist on the western horizon. Far across the valley he could see Yost pulling his canal boat close to the tow-path."[7]

And he can evoke the liveliness of the annual fair at a small upstate village:

> The great day was at hand. The roads to Boonville seethed with people, people in smart buckboards, in frowsy milk wagons, in shining buggies. Horses of all kinds, lean and long, round and fat, mangy and groomed, meek and sour-tempered, crowding all together, kicking and shying, grunting and snorting, but all moving townward. . . . An uninterrupted stream, the people moved in one direction, past booths of drinks, cool and enticing; past the hairy lady's show, that wonderful woman who, with her bare hands, could subdue a "ferocious lion from the jungles" and drag off its decrepit old body "while all the world wondered"; past the glass-blowers' booth and the games of chance. . . . Onward past everything went the crowd, laughing and talking, hurrying on to the grandstand to get good seats. Bustle, confusion, uproar, lurid-colored sweaters, striped pink shirts, hats of straw and hats of felt, hats with berries, hats with flowers, bright orange strawberries, sky-blue roses, all nodding and ducking and moving on, to the grandstand.[8]

Needless to say, Edmonds is best when, in this earliest of his fiction, he draws upon his North Country background; he is less effective when he tries to be too imaginatively romantic, to create a melodramatic tale. Regionalism already seems his forte. Edmonds's collegiate efforts are not uniformly good; but some of the stories are first-rate, not only as the work of an undergraduate apprentice but as that of any serious, mature writer.

Walter D. Edmonds accrued a remarkable number of literary

credits while at Harvard College: diverse short stories and other pieces published in the *Advocate,* and recognition in a national anthology of collegiate writing. He proved already to be a capable follower as well as an admirer of Old Copey.[9] In his first theme for Professor Copeland in English 12 he had submitted a story he called "The End of the Tow-Path." Edmonds's friend, David McCord, recalled later that the story "won the coveted Copeland praise of sounding a brand new note."[10] Edmonds had written basically regional material beginning with "'Jehu'" and "The Last of the Black Dwarfs" in his freshman year, but with the story in Charles Townsend Copeland's class he produced, he said, "what I hoped was a truer picture of upstate canallers, which Scribner's bought at once, though they waited a year to print it."[11] By the time Edmonds returned to "Northlands" the summer of his graduation, with sketches already published in *Forest and Stream* and a Copeland-favored story about to appear in *Scribner's Magazine,* his writing career had been auspiciously launched.

3

Edmonds's Short Stories

THE YEARS WHEN EDMONDS WAS ATTENDING COLLEGE were vibrant ones in American literary history. The 1920s must have been an exciting age to be a student, particularly a student of literature. "Sometime between 1910 and 1920," wrote Professor Robert E. Spiller, "American literature 'came of age,'" and by 1930 when Sinclair Lewis went to Stockholm as the first American recipient of the Nobel Prize for literature, he could announce this coming of age as a fait accompli. "This launching of the second literary renaissance in America," Spiller said, "was a time of youth and change and promise."[1]

Change was everywhere evident. F. Scott Fitzgerald called it the "Jazz Age," Westbrook Pegler tagged it "an era of wonderful nonsense," sports writers hailed it as the "Golden Age," and for everyone it was the "New Era." In literature the critical ferment of the decade following the publication of Van Wyck Brooks's *America's Coming-of-Age* in 1915 created a ripe atmosphere for change. The major movement in criticism, dominated by the literary radicals and neo-humanists, had broken the shackles that had so long bound our writers to nineteenth-century standards and habits.

Fiction was no longer restricted by standards of style and form or limited to predetermined "accepted" subjects; both limitations had pretty much fallen by the wayside. In the short story, too, the rigid plot and polished technique formula writing that had been accepted for decades before in the magazines was on the wane.

As a developing story writer in college, Edmonds tried melodrama, experimented with gothic romance style, and toyed with

25

historical albeit highly imaginative settings; his principal kinship
with any "older tradition," if he had one, was with the local colorists.
The local color movement burgeoned in the latter third of the nineteenth century; its origins lay in those writers who "discovered"
their respective sections of the country, using the peculiarities of locality for all elements of the story—authors like Harriet Beecher
Stowe, Sarah Orne Jewett, and Mary E. Wilkins Freeman for New
England; George Washington Cable, Lafcadio Hearn, and Joel Chan-
dler Harris for the South; and Bret Harte, Edward Eggleston, Hamlin Garland, and Mark Twain for the West and Midwest.

These local colorists had dominated the literary scene for
several decades; with encouragement by the mass circulation magazines the short story became an especially popular genre, though ultimately it, too, became formula, with "characters, situations and
background emasculated for the sake of a tailor-made plot."[2] Edward O'Brien called the period from 1922 to 1930 the "shaping
period." The standardized stories still appeared, with the popular
story becoming "more and more gaseous. A critic had to look more
and more closely to find what he was seeking. But it was there," he
wrote in 1932, "and it was never there before."[3] The maturity that
O'Brien saw in the short story as the thirties opened had been evolv-
ing for some time. In the twenties editor and critic H. L. Mencken
called attention to the commendable lack of "imitative and timo-
rous" dependence upon previous attitudes exhibited by the newer
writers[4]; and, as writers rejected the traditional, the American short
story became indeed "American"—represented by depictions of life
in a small Ohio town for Sherwood Anderson, in the sports arena for
Ring Lardner, in a Mississippi county for William Faulkner, and in
the Mohawk Valley of upstate New York for Walter D. Edmonds.

It was Anderson who served, to use Sculley Bradley's phrase,
as a force and a pioneer for the writers of the 1920s and 1930s. Critics
of the genre tend to concur with Henry Seidel Canby's statement in
Literary History of the United States that Sherwood Anderson had
a "very great influence in liberating the American short story from a
petrifying technique."[5] Anderson's work became the core of a new
Geist for the short story, as his tales in newer periodicals like the
Dial, to which Edmonds would contribute, "were eagerly read by the
young men and women trying to escape the technical tradition of
Poe, Aldrich, and O. Henry, which cramped expression though it
seemed to guarantee financial success."[6] Anderson's "liberating" influence, with his *Winesburg, Ohio* (1919) as a benchmark in literary

history, had become an accomplished fact by the time Edmonds was at work. In many ways, said the editors of a leading short story anthology, "it was a kind of Emancipation Proclamation for American writers." In retrospect, with Sherwood Anderson's kind of writing later almost commonplace, "it is hard to realize," they said, "what a liberating influence he had not only on his contemporaries but on the generations to come after him." In contrast to the formula stories, then still in their ascendency, "Anderson wrote his stories simply, naturally, honestly. It was his placing his stories against a simple, ordinary small-town background that made his work so understandable and so inspiring to other writers."[7] Like Anderson, Edmonds wrote his stories "simply, naturally, honestly"; his prose from college days when he received the praises of Professor Copeland for "sounding a brand new note" was organic and native set. It was, to borrow one of Edward O'Brien's remarks, "substance in which the pulse of life was beating."[8]

THE EARLY SHORT STORIES

It did not take Walter D. Edmonds much more than two or three seasons following graduation to join the roster of established American short story writers. Once outside Harvard he had little difficulty maintaining his already steady pace of writing publishable material. Though he was to be understandably concerned over the low financial rewards that magazine editors were willing to give,[9] he nonetheless devoted his full energies to the genre in which his undergraduate literary efforts had so well groomed him. With a steady stream of his stories finding markets in the leading literary magazines, he seemed right on target. By 1931 four of Edmonds's stories had been reprinted in Edward J. O'Brien's *Best Short Stories* anthologies; within ten years nearly fifty of Edmonds's short stories had been given a one-, two-, or three-star rating by this annual authority on the short story in America.

When Edmonds had finished at college and set his sights on a literary career, he sought the advice of Ellery Sedgwick, the *Atlantic Monthly* editor in Boston, as to whether or not he should take up writing for a living. Sedgwick answered him without hesitation, "Certainly not!" Protesting that he had already done a good deal of writing for the *Advocate* while in college, Edmonds told the *Atlantic* editor, "I think I could do it"; and, despite Sedgwick's indication of the difficulties ahead, Edmonds's persistence had its effect. Sedgwick later recalled that "there was something about the boyish Edmonds that gave me not confidence but hope for confidence. I asked him to leave the scripts he had brought, and told him to come back a week later." That evening Ellery Sedgwick read Edmonds's story "The Voice of the Archangel." "Something there is about talent," he said, "that gives color even to an ill-typed page. I could hardly miss this, and though I did not see in my mind's eye the advertisement of half a million copies of *Drums Along the Mohawk* by Walter D. Edmonds, all serious doubt disappeared."[10]

The story Sedgwick had reviewed, "The Voice of the Archangel," appeared in the January 1928 *Atlantic*. A story in the repertoire of one of Edmonds's most enduring characters—Lucy Cashdollar, who ran her Cooks' Agency for Bachelor Boaters on the canals of New York State—this tale was the first of five Edmonds's short stories to be published in the *Atlantic* in the next year and a half. Moreover, the short fiction of Edmonds also appeared in a number of other leading periodicals, among them the *Dial, Harper's Magazine, The Forum* (later *The Forum and Century*), and *Scribner's Magazine.* Except for the sketches he sold to *Forest and Stream*, it was *Scribner's* that had the distinction of first publishing Edmonds, outside of the *Advocate*, when they accepted his story, "The End of the Tow-Path"; the story, sent with Professor Copeland's blessing, appeared when Edmonds had been out of college barely a month.

In this story of an old, retired canal boater, Mark, and his partner on the canal, Samson Hanks, Edmonds depicts a nostalgic tragedy of a bygone age. The two men had murdered a bank carrier forty years before, but it was Hanks who went to jail for all those years, not for the murder but actually "with something else against him." Old Mark had the money, the freedom, and his memories. The reunion of the two canallers after Hanks's forty-year sentence is up proved to be the beginning of the end for both of the old-timers. This initial story contains elements which will in one way or another appear in countless others. At one point, as Mark ponders the solution to his peculiar and personal problem, Edmonds describes a scene which foreshadows similar ones in story and novel, a scene that is indigenously authentic and which also vividly and poignantly catches the feeling of his character and of the era that has passed.

From where he sat he could see the valley of the Black River winding northward for miles. The water shone with a purple light, and the wind plucked up a ripple in a gleam, dazzling as diamonds. The farmers were drawing in the corn, the teams plodding heavily, well set against the collars, while the tall bundles rose in the arms of the men and swung upward and over upon the racks with the regularity of automatons. He could hear the chugging of a gasoline-engine half a mile away, and even catch the whistle and the long sigh as the knives bit through the stalks and the fan blew the ensilage into the silo.

Upon his left, near the tops of the hills, the feed-canal ran just below him. He could trace its downward course across the divide to the beginning of the Lansing Kill, where it dropped through forty locks in ten miles, before it reached the Delta Basin, to move on slowly to the Erie Canal. From there, he remembered, the latter moved on, with all its locks to Rome and Utica and Syracuse, until it ran past Geneseo, all the way to Buffalo and the lakes. In his mind's eye he saw the cities, too, and followed the ghostly shadow of the towpath to their oyster booths and bars. While he mused, he thought the boats came out upon the water, laden down with heavy cargoes, and the steersmen leaned on the sweeps, while the great rudders brought them slowly round the bends; and one boat tripped its rope for another to pass, while the crews laughed and jollied in the passing. With the coming of night, lights shone suddenly at intervals along the banks, and he was privileged to climb their gang-walks aboard, to sit by the open grates in the cabins and smoke, to drink warm rum from the heavy steins and to sleep deep sleeps again, with the water gurgling close to his ear and the soft swish of water grass weaving him dreams. A great longing rose up in his heart to be again what he once had been. . . .

The sun was low upon the horizon when he awoke and raised his head. He looked down the canal, but it was empty; and he knew that he had dreamed—that the boats, the horses, and the men, that the canal, with its solitary companion towpath, had run to their end; and that he was alone upon the hill—a last, withered owl, perched by the hand of fate upon a dead branch in his dying tree.

Within the year, *Scribner's Magazine* accepted and published a second Edmonds short story, "Who Killed Rutherford?" In 1928 they published a third, "Duet in September." The first sees Solomon Tinkle and Mrs. Gurget, characters in other Edmonds pieces, discussing who might have "done in" the owner of a line of bars and posthouses between Utica and Syracuse. Even Jotham Klore makes an offstage appearance in Solomon Tinkle's telling how one of the girls, Nancy Haskins, was riled at Rutherford and auctioned herself off to Klore for three hundred dollars, and how Klore became bar-keep in Bentley's Oyster Bar and Booth in Utica, which Rutherford had acquired.

"Duet in September," the next *Scribner's* story, is the por-trait of an elderly couple, old John Adam and his wife, Eve, sitting side by side in their rockers on their front porch one Sunday after-noon. As he reads of the execution of one of their boys, John Adams reminisces of the forty-two years since he bought his first boat with the money his tight-fisted uncle, Amos Gives, had left him; of Eve, taken out of a Methodist orphanage by Mrs. Jennings as a maid; of the years he and Eve spent on the *Nancy Gives* before they were married, and the other years on the farm after they had gone into the church on Genesee Street in Utica as John and Eve and come out man and wife. And there was the apple, too, or, rather, both of them: the one at the Jennings farm long ago which Eve took a bite out of and passed to John by way of saying "yes," and the one now, the first one raised from their own farm tree.

> Carefully he held it out to her. It was not a very big apple; but she took it and looked at it, smelled of it to please him.
> "It smells sweet," she said.
> "Taste it, Eve."
> She had a bite.
> "It tastes sweet."
> She bit into it again.
> "Here," said John Adam. "Let me have it. You can't eat it all, Eve."
> He took it from her, munched it, got rid of a seed which he snapped over the porch rail.
> "It's a good apple, Eve. It's real sweet."

Each of these stories is an Anderson kind of story, though this is not to say they are not uniquely Edmonds. Each is a study of behavior, to paraphrase Canby's assessment of Anderson,[11] realisti-cally handled, though not for the sake of realism, and of sympathy for the characters and the times, though neither defending or judg-ing them.

Edmonds kept the stories coming. The *Dial* carried "The

Swamper" in its March 1928 issue, and the *Atlantic Monthly* published five stories in 1928 and 1929. In all these stories Edmonds continued to deal with regional characters in regional settings. "The Swamper," for example, is another former boater story whose central figure has "gone twirly," as the canal vernacular describes him. He was kept on as a clean-up man ("Sweeps the barroom for two meals a day and sleeps in the mill barn . . ."). The locale is Amos Gives's saloon on the Black River Canal, the same Amos Gives whose nephew, John Adam, Edmonds presented in "Duet in September." "The Voice of the Archangel," the first Edmonds story to appear in the *Atlantic,* features one of the girls from Mrs. Cashdollar's Cooks' Agency for Bachelor Boaters. May Friendly hired out on the *Eastern Belle,* where the two Glenn brothers who own the boat vie for her affection, much to the amused interest of their old friend, an itinerant cigar peddler named Harvey Cannywhacker. With observer figures like Cannywhacker, conversations about dairying versus canalling, and complications arising out of one of the Glenn's troubling interest in moving to the Ohio country to take up dairy farming, this story (as with a number of others published during the author's immediate postcollege period) contains elements of character, situation, and setting that are to turn up again in *Rome Haul* and subsequent writing.

But while in these and other short stories the author continued to deal principally with the everyday, often somber affairs of regional characters in indigenous settings, there were other facets to Edmonds's writing yet to surface. One of the early *Atlantic Monthly* stories, "Death of Red Peril," and a 1932 story, "The Cruise of the Cashalot," which appeared in another periodical, illustrate Edmonds's enduring interest in animal life as well as in folklore. There were hints of this interest and Edmonds's special way of telling a tale in even his earliest undergraduate writing, when he told the story of the fabulous "Black Maria." He has a unique talent, molded doubtless by his boyhood experiences at "Northlands" among farmers, former canallers, and sundry other country types, that couples with his intrinsic storyteller's instincts to make memorable for his audience a dog, a horse, a cow, an Adirondack black bear, or even a caterpillar.

"Death of Red Peril," for instance, is the story of a caterpillar. It's a racing caterpillar, the pride of its owner. Typical of the times when cock fighting, dog fighting, and other such "amusements" characterized the country scene, this *Atlantic* short story has become one of Edmonds's most anthologized pieces. A red, long-haired caterpillar that was picked up somewhere along the country road to Westernville, Red Peril must have been descended, some said, from the caterpillars Paul Bunyan used to race. As Edmonds begins his tale, he lets his narrator explain the racing technique to the reader:

> The way we raced caterpillars was to set them in a napkin ring on a table, one facing one way and one the other. Outside the napkin ring was drawed a circle in chalk three feet acrost. Then a man lifted the ring and the handlers was allowed one jab with a darning needle to get their caterpillars started. The one that got outside the chalk circle the first was the one that won the race.

Red Peril turned out to be the fastest caterpillar in seven counties. The story and the caterpillar appealed enough to C. S. Thomas to assure its inclusion in his representative volume of *Modern Atlantic Stories* in 1932; Edmonds put it in his own short story collection *Mostly Canallers* two years later, and the tale's popularity grew. At least one critic of historical fiction has suggested that Red Peril deserves to be mentioned with Mark Twain's celebrated jumping frog of Calaveras County.[12]

Perhaps even more closely associated with American folklore and the tall tale side of American culture is Edmonds's "The Cruise of the Cashalot," a short story which first ran in *The Forum and Century*. This story marked the beginning of the literary life of a remarkable whale that was rammed by a tug in New York harbor and later exhibited almost the full length of the Erie Canal by an enterprising boater.[13] Like Edmonds's caterpillar tale and countless other stories, this imaginative folk yarn drew upon regional practice and folklore; in fact, "The Cruise of the Cashalot" was inspired, partly at least, by Edmonds's hearing of an actual whale exhibit on the Erie Canal. "Someone told me," Edmonds explained in a note in the *New York Folklore Quarterly,* "that a canaller had stabbed a whale in the eye on his way across the (New York) Harbor and then exhibited it up the Hudson and the Canal as far as Rome where they could no longer get the swollen carcass under the bridges. All the rest of my rigamarole burgeoned from that."[14]

The story unfolds in typical folktale style as the narrator sits down to jaw a bit with a fellow logger named John. One learns at the outset that John's Uncle Ben Meekum ("a kind of dingy old coot") was a canaller who had been living a pretty henpecked existence. When he married Aunt Em, John said, "the two of them made just about the most respectable kind of home life a woman could want. Uncle Ben would load his boat, and him and Henry Plat, who done his driving, would get the old boat along with the aid of Ben's mules; but inside the boat the old lady ruled the roost." But Aunt Em took pride in the boat even if it was Ben's. She'd fixed it up fine, and the curtained windows had "the best geraniums on the Erie." When Em received a letter telling her that her Ma had sugar diabetes, she had to leave Uncle Ben to freight it alone down to New York City. This proved to be a dramatic turning point in their lives, beginning when Uncle Ben's boat, the *Louisa*, rammed a whale in New York harbor.

"What," says the driver to Ben, "are you going to do with a whale?" Henry Plat reminded Ben that Aunt Em would "squeak" him good when she found out about such goings on. "Em," snorted Uncle Ben, "hasn't got nothing to say about this whale." He later explained his plan to load the whale aboard the *Louisa* and take her up the Erie Canal. And that's just what he did. The whale was hoisted on board the boat with her nose on the cabin roof and her tail hanging over the front end. They dug out the innards to allow for a bar and a refreshment parlor, Ben figuring with entrepreneurial savvy, "I'd ought to get the ladies and children, too." When he had the *Louisa* exhibit full-rigged, it made some spectacle going up the canal:

> They had kind of washed her outside but she looked a little greasy; but, as Uncle Ben said, everybody had seen a bullhead boat anyway. It was the whale they'd look at. And sure enough, there was the whale stretched out on the boat, looking Uncle Ben right in the eye where he stood steering. She had a door in her side opposite the gang, and a flag stuck into her nose saying CASHALOT in green letters. And over the door was a sign saying, "Be a Jonah for fifty cents." And underneath it said, "Complete equipment."

Uncle Ben even added a pair of glasses from an oculist's shop. Before he reached Rome, New York, about halfway along the Erie to Buffalo, Ben had made more than a thousand dollars. Farmers came from fifty miles around to look at Ben's whale. But as the weather grew hotter the whale began to swell, and this forced Ben to trim it in order to get under the Erie's low bridges. As Ben trimmed he had to cut the price of admission. By the time Aunt Em returned to the canal boat, however, the receipts that Uncle Ben had taken in impressed her, since even Aunt Em could see that Uncle Ben was a heroic whalekiller not scared of a woman any more. Ben asserted himself, sold the whale for fertilizer for eighty cents when they reached Rochester on the canal, and told Em to clean up the boat. She did, too. Afterward, she and Uncle Ben led a happy life on the geranium-pretty *Louisa*. Aunt Em not only no longer objected to Ben's occasional drinking, she joined him! "Once she'd been unloosed by whiskey," the storyteller lets on, "she turned out to be a fond woman."

This delightful "rigamarole," as Edmonds termed it, proved good enough to have "The Cruise of the Cashalot" selected for the 1932 O. Henry Memorial Award prize stories anthology and to reappear in Edmonds's book *Mostly Canallers* two years hence. In regard to the story's title, the change of the single letter in the French *cachalot*, a kind of whale, to the Erie Canal boater's "cashalot" is both humorously inventive and realistic, for to the average mid-nineteenth-century American "cashalot" was an easy confusion. One should not dismiss Edmonds's gentle satire either. When Ben checks the public library to try to find out what kind of whale he has, he finds there are at least fourteen varieties. He tells his driver, Henry Plat, that this is a "cash-a-lot." "My God," says Henry, "maybe there is money in her, after all." Certainly, in terms of the entrepreneurial hero, cashalot makes a good deal of sense. One editor suggested that Edmonds borrowed the title, "with the difference of a significant letter," from Frank T. Bullen's *The Cruise of the Cachalot*, which dealt with an actual whaleman's adventures at sea; but she praised Edmonds the storyteller: compare, if you will, she says, with Mr. Bullen, but "the chances are that the factual events . . . will be received with no more credulity than this whopper, this wholly satisfactory fiction."[15] At any rate, Bullen aside, Edmonds's whale would appear to have close literary and folklore antecedents in Mark Twain, the frontier humorists of the nineteenth century, and Paul Bunyan tales. It has considerable kinship, also, with the tradition of P. T. Barnum and, closer to home, to such upstate New York lore as the Cardiff Giant hoax that in 1869 had all kinds of people, from farmers to professors, flocking to Stubb Newell's Onondaga County farm to view the mighty "discovery."[16]

EDMONDS COLLECTED: *MOSTLY CANALLERS*

In 1934 twenty-four of Edmonds's stories dealing with upstate New York characters and locales were published in a collection of his own that was appropriately titled *Mostly Canallers*. This book, a generous potpourri of canal life and lore, with an occasional nonnautical character thrown in for good measure, faithfully depicts an era and a region for which the author was rapidly becoming a chief literary spokesman. Episodic and anecdotal, these stories catch in various ways something of the nuances of real life as it was in the days when the Erie Canal offered a passage west for many travelers and settlers, and a livelihood in upstate New York towns and villages for countless other persons. The common denominator of the stories is humanism. The fighting, brawling, and general tempestuousness of the times when western New York was still very much a real frontier are recaptured in *Mostly Canallers;* but the stories show the serious side of living in those days and the tragedy also, as well as the sentimentality that today is only a kind of historic nostalgia.

"Upstate New York has provided Walter D. Edmonds with an inexhaustible store of characters one would like to know," said the editors of the *Atlantic Monthly* in regard to one of the stories reprinted there[17]; and "*Mostly Canallers* presents a goodly array of people in an equally wide variety of situations. Some of the characters Edmonds writes of—like Jotham Klore, Mrs. Gurget, the Irishman O'Mory, or Lucy Cashdollar—recur in other pieces of Edmonds's writing, including his early stories in the *Advocate*. Some, on the other hand, are uniquely set in the particular episode in which one meets them, for there is no counterpart nor precedent to the author's so sympathetically drawn figures of young Eve Winslow and Perry Joslin, who marry on the canal, and John and Eve Adams, who look back on more than forty years together.

In subject matter the tales Edmonds tells range from this same naive "sparking" of the seventeen-year-old Eve and Perry Joslin, "tall and gawky as a heron" and "the craziest lock-tender in the Kill Gorge," in "Blind Eve," to the fearful times of the cholera scourge that hit upstate New York in the 1830s, as told in "The Old Jew's Tale."[18] In time they range from the beginning of the canal days, "Citizens for Ohio" and "At Schoharie Crossing," to "The End of the Tow-Path." Edmonds's characters in *Mostly Canallers* include

Cover design for the first edition of Walter D. Edmonds's short story collection, *Mostly Canallers*. Reproduced by permission of Little, Brown and Company.

many persons who remain more or less anonymous, but they represent real people who lived in the times—those who are bound for the Ohio country or other new homesteads via the Eria Canal; redemptioner servants who happily meet friendly travelers and sometimes prospective husbands along the way; old people with reminiscences of an insecure youth, and young ones with a zest for the adventures canalling offered.

Mostly Canallers contains a number of stories already discussed in this chapter: the first three *Scribner's Magazine* stories ("The End of the Tow-Path," "Who Killed Rutherford?" and "Duet in September"), "The Swamper" from the *Dial*, two of his earliest *Atlantic* stories ("The Voice of the Archangel" and "Death of Red Peril"), and "The Cruise of the Cashalot."

All these and many others in *Mostly Canallers* depict the times and concerns of the boaters expertly and authentically. A tale like "At Schoharie Crossing" reveals much about the folkways of the Canal Era in America, but also provides the reader with historically valid insight into the real problems our forebears faced as they traveled the canals of early America. In the story sixty boats are drawn up on the towpath at the Schoharie Crossing, waiting for the raging waters of the creek just beyond Schenectady, New York, to abate so the canal boats can make a safe crossing. As the storyteller explains it:

> In those first years of the Erie, the crossing stream was let into the canal on one side, with a guard lock below, and a dam on the other side to take the overflow along its natural channel. It was easy enough to cross above the dam with the water at normal level; but when a freshet hit a creek, the space above the dam became a mill race, with treacherous eddies to add trouble to the side pull. There were plenty of such crossings on the Old Erie, but the Schoharie was the worst of the lot. [P. 30]

Waiting strained everybody's nerves, and, as often on the canal, such waiting, whether for normal lockage or crossing such as this in bad weather, led to fighting. In this case it is Herman Peters, the Utica bully, who insists that no one pass ahead of his boat. "Since she come on the Erie, the *Pretty Fashion* ain't never been second on any lock she come to," says Peters. An Irishman named O'Mory—perhaps the very same O'Mory who later appears in Edmonds's'1933 novel, *Erie Water,* during the canal construction—offers a challenge from his *Dublin Queen;* but it is young Dan Wagner ("Dan Wagner . . . a young man going west!") who takes on the bully. Impatient with anyone or anything that stands in the way of his getting to Ohio in time for the planting season, Dan overcomes both obstacles, the bully and the crossing. The latter causes the most comment. "You're a stranger on this canal," said one of canallers,"or you'd know it couldn't be did." When Dan says he has a good team, an-

An ink sketch of a tranquil canal scene used as the end papers illustration for Walter D. Edmonds's *Mostly Canallers*. Reproduced by permission of Little, Brown and Company.

other canaller tells him: "'Maybe you have,' said Joe; 'but the last four boats that tried crossing on high water went over the dam. One took three mules with it, and the rope broke on the others.' 'I got a new rope, and my team ain't mules'" (p. 39). After beating Peters, Dan Wagner crosses with his team. As he starts off westward, O'Mory and the others strain their eyes to read the name painted on the back of Wagner's boat. A traveler takes out a small telescope and reads out the letters: "S-U-R-E A-R-R-I-V-A-L. 'Thank ye, sir,'" says O'Mory.

General mayhem-making, including brawling, seems to have been natural to canal life, though some say the largest part of it was created by fiction writers. Folklorists and cultural historians, however, tend to uphold the basic validity of such literary versions of canal life as depicted in an Edmonds tale or in those of Herbert Quick, whom Edmonds read, and Samuel Hopkins Adams, whose forebears were canallers.[19] At any rate, Erie literature, including newspaper accounts, keeps the legend of the fighting canaller alive. Among the stories in *Mostly Canallers,* "Water Never Hurt a Man" gives us an incident in which George Brace, bully of the Black River Canal, takes on Buffalo Joe Buller, a Canadian who was the bully of the western end of the Erie. George's son John earns his manhood, too, when their boat, the *Bacconola,* is waiting at the lock one stormy night. "Who Killed Rutherford?" finds a brawler from Edmonds's *Advocate* fiction reappearing, though the later "bully of the Erie Canal" in the novel *Rome Haul* does no onstage fighting in this tale: as noted earlier, he becomes a barkeep in Utica. There's a brawling incident, though, in "Citizens for Ohio," which concerns a teamster who feels that the new Erie Canal, which opened in 1825, may ruin team hauling. He runs into a redemptioner and decides to move on. Like the Wagners who successfully navigated the Schoharie Crossing, he heads for Ohio.

In contrast, mild-mannered men and women also have their day in *Mostly Canallers.* In "Mr. Dennit's Great Adventure" a warehouse clerk finds himself for the first time in his routine existence in the midst of a life-and-death situation on one of the setbacks in the Blacksnake region of the Erie's middle stretches. His unnerving experience has an uncommon ending—he is saved by a nude girl on her wedding eve! In "An Honest Deal" a horse-trader by the unlikely but real name of I. Finis Wilson[20] unceremoniously goes about selling off a dead horse, collecting a $100 profit, and maintaining his honor in doing it. It is a first-rate story of brains over brawn in the best of camp fire tall tale tradition. So, too, is "The Cruise of the Cashalot," discussed earlier in this chapter, in which the meekly submissive Uncle Ben Meekum becomes master of his household after some shenanigans with a dead whale onboard his Erie Canal bullhead boat.

Then there's Big-Foot Sal, a middle-aged, gin-drinking, good Samaritan sort of woman whose name evokes the folklore of the canalling days, for Sal may very well have been inspired by the boater's cook in the many versioned ballad:

> The cook we had on board the deck stood six feet in her socks;
> Her hand was like an elephant's ear, her breath would open
> the locks.[21]

Edmonds's Sal is not a caricature, however, and he elicits sympathy for her in the reader. The story "Big-Foot Sal" shows how this

woman who always wanted to have a baby and never had one plays
midwife to a sister canaller on the Long Level, a long, flat stretch of
Erie water from Salina to Rome. The story opens with the anxiety
aboard George and Opal's canal boat *Ohio;* the time is just before the
winter closing of the canal and "the clop of the mules' hoofs in the
half-frozen mud" the only sound the driver hears. Opal, due with
child, is in labor earlier than George had hoped, for he thought they
would have time to make Lucy Cashdollar's place in Utica. ("Lucy
took care of her girls that way," Edmonds tells us, referring to the
fact that anyone who signed on an Erie boat through Mrs. Cashdollar's Cooks' Agency for Bachelor Boaters was a client for life if
she wanted; she had a kind of built-in health plan as part of her contract.) When the *Ohio* had passed the last lighted farmhouse, no
other haven could be seen on that stretch of canal, and the old *Ohio*
seemed to be the last boat hauling on the Long Level. Then in the
Erie wilderness Ben the driver hears a boat coming west. It was like
a miracle to George. Stopping the other boat, George asked if a
woman was aboard. A gnomelike old man, Cooney, answered across
the water,

> "Well, I have."
> "Can she come over? My girl's in trouble."
> "What is it?"
> "Baby."

George jumped into the water to go fetch her from the other side of
the Erie. By the time he reached the opposite berm he saw her, a
broad, squat figure stomping along the towpath. As Edmonds describes her, George saw "a middle-aged woman with hair of indeter-
minate color straggling from under her shawl, and the biggest feet
he had ever seen. Her eyes were bleary and her breath whistled; but
she looked like an angel. . . ." "I'll do the whole thing," Sal says to
George, as he carried her across the canal to his boat and led her to
the sleeping cuddy.

  Later, Cooney tells George how it is with him and Sal. "Sal
don't look so good," Cooney says, "but she's the best damn cook on
the Erie Canal." And he told how this awkward-appearing woman
with the big feet and saintly qualities never had the child she
wanted: "She's always wanted a baby. Funny thing—here she is forty-
four years old and every year she wants it worse. There wouldn't

nobody else hire her on." Playing midwife to Opal that night would upset her bad; no doubt it would play "billy-bubs"with Sal's works, Cooney said to George.

The collection helped to bring Edmonds's writing before new readers, for *Mostly Canallers* put some of his best regional stories into one handy package for book readers to enjoy. There's variety enough; yet each story in its own way sheds a bit of understanding on a region and its history, its people. Today many of them would seem to be old-fashioned, but they ought never to be out of style.

SENIOR SHORT STORY WRITER

Right from the beginning, Edmonds's stories gained recognition in national anthologies. Edward J. O'Brien, whose *Best Short Stories of 1926* gave "The End of the Tow-Path" its highest rating, followed by choosing "The Swamper" from the *Dial* for his 1928 edition. In 1929, 1931, and 1933, three more of Edmonds's short stories—"Death of Red Peril," already discussed; "Water Never Hurt a Man," which originally appeared in *Harper's Weekly;* and "Black Wolf," a *Saturday Evening Post* story—were reprinted among O'Brien's annual "best."

Thus Ellery Sedgwick's early suspicion of the young writer's talent proved to be highly valid; and Edmonds's reputation grew steadily in nationally circulated periodicals. In addition to the O'Brien anthologies, his work in this magazine field soon was being reprinted in such collections as *Modern Atlantic Stories* (1932), *A Book of the Short Story* (1934), and the *O. Henry Memorial Award Prize Stories* collections (editions of 1932, 1934, and 1936). After 1935 Edmonds was also represented in the annual *Post Stories* series.

Whether Edmonds was fashioning an entire story around an episode in the folk past or reviving the rich heritage of New York State and its culture and people, he has provided tales that are frequently highly entertaining as well as being historically authentic. He serves up the folk legendry of the American Revolution, for example, in "Indian Running" (1936), wherein a colonial scout outruns the Indians to warn Fort Herkimer of an impending attack by the Indian marauders under Joseph Brant; and he brings to life the Helderberg story of Trudy Van Alstyne in "The Spanish Gun" (1937), which illustrates his typical utilization of the folk past in retelling a story for modern readers. "The Spanish Gun" is the story of how Trudy became the best *spinster* in the Helderberg Mountains. "When a young girl had learned to spin and had done her proper stint," Edmonds explained in an author's note to the *Saturday Evening Post* story, "she was called a spinster and was considered eligible for marriage." Trudy's fame as a spinster, he said, "has been handed down until our own day to her great-great-great-grandson, Thomas R. Shepherd, of Ilion, New York, who has told me."[22] This concern for tradition and history became more and more evident in Edmonds's work, both in stories and longer fiction, for he is equally at home dealing with upstate New York farmers during the Revolutionary War, builders of the Erie Canal or boaters who rode upon it, New York City merchants in the age of Andrew Jackson, or restless young people living with a circus, crewing aboard a merchantman on the high seas, or even a Confederate lad in an observation balloon during the Civil War.

Edmonds's stories continued also to reflect his high regard for nature and animal life, fostered by his knowledge of farm life and his hunting experiences around "Northlands." Dog stories like "Honor of the County" (1933) and horse stories like "The First Race of Blue Dandy" and "The White-Nosed Colt" (both in 1934) are first-rate animal stories. In "Perfection of Orchard View" (1934) his subject is prize hogs! His story about an old hound dog named Moses is something else again: in "Moses," published in the *Atlantic Monthly* in 1938, the storyteller delightfully combines fact with inventive fiction. Like the whale and caterpillar stories, "Moses" is pure entertainment, with a dash of tongue-in-cheek satire thrown in, as characters such as Saint Peter, Daniel Boone, Kit Carson, and "a man named Francis from Assisi" try to assist a hound dog's entrance into Heaven.

What happens, Edmonds asks, to an inveterate North Country hunting hound who can no longer chase the fox? His fictional dog is based upon a real hound that Edmonds knew, one he had hunted with from the village store in Hawkinsville, some few miles from the Edmonds's place. In "Moses" he imagines the difficulty the poor departed hound has in meeting with the Committee on Admissions at the Pearly Gates, for staring the dog in the face upon his arrival is the sign:

TAKE NOTICE

NO
DOGS
SORCERERS
WHOREMONGERS
MURDERERS
IDOLATORS
LIARS
WILL BE
ADMITTED

But the country hound dog persists, and various figures help Moses out, or "in" perhaps one ought to say. Important among these helpful and charitable characters is an ordinary Yorker, Freem Brock, who startles the celestial ears by stating in no uncertain language that a Heaven that kept out Moses was one hell of a place! The story subsequently has found its way into short story collections as one of Edmonds's more enduring pieces; and it was selected for inclusion in *Jubilee*, the centennial volume of representative writings from the *Atlantic*.[23]

Throughout the 1930s Edmonds's name was linked again and again, especially in the pages of the *Saturday Evening Post*, with those of other successful and popular literary figures. Out of Edmonds's association with the *Post* during these years was also to come a rather impressive number of books for younger readers, ones which had titles like *Two Logs Crossing* (1945), *They Had a Horse* (1962), *Tom Whipple* (1942), and *Wilderness Clearing* (1949): these all had their origin as *Post* short stories. In addition, the novel *Red Wheels Rolling* (later issued in book form as *Chad Hanna*) appeared serially in the *Post*, as did portions of *Drums Along the Mohawk* and stories like "Honor of the County" and pieces about a Horatio Alger kind of young hero named John Ames that later formed parts of larger works.[24]

By far the majority of Edmonds's short fiction went to the *Post* during this period. "What his Ph.D. is to the scholar, the acceptance of a manuscript by the *Saturday Evening Post* is to a short story writer" is the way one of the dust jacket blurbs stated the case on the collection of *Post Stories of 1935*, the pilot volume in what became a well-known and reputable anthology series. Edmonds had by this time already earned the right to be called by *Post* editors one of the magazine's "senior fiction writers," along with Stephen Vincent Benét, Booth Tarkington, and other familiar literary names of the decade. The 1935 *Post Stories* mentioned above contained "Judge," one of Edmonds's best youth-learning-life stories; and represented in the collection with Edmonds—there were twenty-one stories in all —were such authors as Benét, T. S. Stribling, John P. Marquand, and the rising Paul Gallico. When "Judge" originally appeared in the *Post* pages, the editors rightly referred to it as "one of the most powerful short stories this author has devised."[25]

This story about John Haskell, as the author later described it, tells basically "how and why a boy grew up to become the man he did. It is a very simple story, and it is concerned partly with what other people did for John, but mostly with what John did for himself." This was in the foreword to a book edition of the short story, published as *Two Logs Crossing* in 1945. The latter title derives from the woodsman's practice of felling two trees to cross an open stream. Seth, an Indian who teaches John Haskell the art of trapping, put it this way: "If creeks open, you cut two logs crossing. You mind Seth. You cut two logs. One log roll. Two logs safe crossing water." In general, this story, as so many of Edmonds's pieces, was essentially a true one. "As a matter of fact," said Edmonds, "every man who has ever made anything of his life has had to earn to use two logs where two logs are needed. There is no trick and easy way to independence, either for a man or a country."[26]

Another *Post* story of the period, "Tom Whipple, the Acorn, and the Emperor of Russia" (1939), shows the author's growing interest in the theme of youth and maturity in young America, a concern which is also reflected in novels like *Chad Hanna, Erie Water,* and *Young Ames,* and novelettes like *Cadmus Henry.* The story about Tom Whipple appeared originally in the *Post* issue for September 25, 1939; it was reprinted in Alexander Woollcott's wartime collection, *As You Were* (1941), and later selected as one of a group of representative American stories in *A Treasury of Short Stories* (1948), edited by Bernadine Kielty. Dodd, Mead published *Tom Whipple* as a separate book in 1942; and Little, Brown reprinted it in *Seven American Stories* in 1970.

Tom Whipple is a Yankee lad, born in New Haven; at the time of the story he hails from Westernville in York State ("It's just north of Rome," he says), where Tom's father had moved the family from Connecticut. Edmonds's story is a retelling of an American legend first recorded by Maria Child in 1840. In Edmonds's story Tom Whipple, determined to see the world, goes from the Mohawk Valley to the palace of the Russian emperor, Nicholas II, proving during the course of this simple yet eloquent tale, that "any American lad, like Tom Whipple here, can get along anywhere on earth." A good reason for this philosophy, as the author wrote in his preface to the book version, lies in the maxim that the Yankee long ago "learned he was good as the next if he believed he was, and if he wasn't beholden to anyone." Tom Whipple's story is essentially the story of America itself.

Set in the time of President Martin Van Buren, the short story opens with Tom, returning from a visit to "Washington City" and Mount Vernon, seeing his mother off on the Albany steamer, and going about to find a job. When he signs onboard the ship *Flora Bascom* bound for St. Petersburg, he is rudely inducted into the anything but romantic common seaman's life:

> Tom Whipple felt the *Flora Bascom*'s forefoot take the heave of the Atlantic, and he saw the dirty green of its restless waste meeting a steel-grey sky. The cries of the tagging gulls lost heart and dwindled. By evening the brig was a lonely box on the waves with eighteen men and a spotted cat, and America was a place on which the sun had set.

Edmonds's style is sure. In metaphor images ("He felt the back wind off the sails against his face; the curve of them made dingy feather beds to lure a man to let go . . .") and similes (". . . he tried looking down and saw the hull slitting the water like a needle that a bug might straddle"), Edmonds depicts the young man's reactions to his adventure at sea, where he is buffeted by wind and gale, and by the driving orders of the mate who keeps him riding high in the rigging ("Maybe the wind will blow the hayseed out").

Tom Whipple personifies Yankee youth, with a curious Puritan strain of independence, pragmatic yet not materialistic. He thought of his mother's concern about him: "'He didn't have any money,' he thought of his mother's saying: 'He didn't want any. You know how Tom is. Always going around with his pocket full of nails and things he picks up, thinking he is as good as the richest man alive.'" And the more he thought about the *Flora Bascom*'s destination, the more determined he became to visit the emperor—"Always go the man at the top," Tom's father's friend used to tell him—and the way in which Tom Whipple boyishly seeks and succeeds in gaining an audience with the emperor combines an indigenous American naiveté with an equally characteristic directness of mind and action.

The interview between Tom and Mr. Dallas, the American diplomatic minister, also typifies Edmonds's belief that the best way of getting things done is the ordinary, straightforward, and simple way:

> Mr. Dallas looked at him for a moment before he said, picking his words, "You know, Whipple, the Emperor's a pretty hard man to get to see." Then he tried to explain how it was in an empire as compared to a democratic country. Tom thought it over, but shook his head. He said he couldn't see it that way. He could see it might apply to a Russian farmer, in a manner of speaking; but he was a United States citizen. Martin Van Buren, now, he could see the Emperor, couldn't he? Mr. Dallas nodded his head; that was true. Then why couldn't Tom Whipple?
>
> Well, they sawed away at it for a spell, and Mr. Dallas was as friendly a man as you could ask to argue with. But Tom got the best of him at every turn, and finally he agreed to write a letter to the Imperial Court Chamberlain for Tom. But he said there was one thing: it was the custom when you went to call on an emperor to take him a present.
>
> Tom hadn't thought of that but he could see how it could be, and he stuck his hand in his pants' pocket to fiddle with the junk he carried, the way he always did when he was puzzled, and his fingers closed on an object he'd hardly thought of since leaving Washington City. Holding it, he thought how lucky it was he hadn't dropped it anywhere, like up on the topsail yards . . .
>
> "All right," he said. "Tell him I got a present I'd mighty like to give the Emperor and that I figure the Emperor is going to be mighty pleased to have."

Tom's gift of a simple acorn, picked up at Mount Vernon, strikes an amused and responsive chord in the czar of all the Russians. "I thought you'd appreciate it," Tom tells him, "being it comes from the home of the greatest man of the U.S.A., greater even than Old Hickory." In their ensuing discussion one sees Edmonds's humanism at work, with as unlikely a cast as one can imagine in these days of SALT agreements and cold wars: a Russian emperor who admitted he couldn't always do what he wanted but had to stick to his day-to-day job "by and large, to get along, just like an ordinary man," and a Yankee youth who could point out sincerely that "even an ordinary man had to work like an Emperor." This illustrates well what Walter D. Edmonds's fiction often is saying: the things that bind people together far outweigh those that divide them.

Edmonds's short stories are in the best tradition of the storyteller's art, for they are stories—not experiments in technique, not contrivances in support of some particular literary mode or aesthetic theory. They surely belong more to the oral storytelling tradition than to any written one of form and structure. They are close to the people—the folk—and to the natural environment with whom and with which they deal. Thematically, these short stories are all concerned with people; they and Edmonds's longer works share the same Yorker-based philosophy of individual worth and dignity, of commonsense approaches to the problems of living, and of simple pleasures which sometimes show how very close sadness is to laughter, tragedy to comedy.

4

Rome Haul and the Canal Novel

$\mathcal{A}$ FTER RECEIVING HIS BACHELOR OF ARTS DEGREE in June 1926, Edmonds returned to the family home, "Northlands," where he wrote a bit and pondered the possibilities of a literary career. While that first year after his graduation from college resulted in a fair sheaf of stories, it was painfully obvious that a successful writing career had to return something more substantial than the few initially marketable short stories promised. "I think they added up to about nine hundred dollars, which isn't much of an income," Walter remarked about his short story efforts in the first year after Cambridge.[1] His interest in tackling longer fiction, especially a novel which would draw upon his Boonville farm experience and his knowledge of canal boatmen on the Black River Canal and the Erie Canal offered the opportunity he needed.

At the urging of Professor Copeland and of Ellery Sedgwick, the *Atlantic Monthly* editor, Edmonds turned enthusiastically to writing a book. The effort paid off; the result was a novel about the Erie Canal period which he called *Rome Haul.*

In numerous short stories and in two novels and a novelette the Grand Canal of New York State—the Erie—provided Edmonds with major theme and setting. If the canal and its canallers are considered in their larger influence, there is hardly a work by Edmonds which did not in some way reflect the effects of his Black River Valley boyhood and his deep rooted interest in the days of the old Erie. Like Samuel Hopkins Adams, who followed Edmonds in creating a successful genre out of the canal novel, Edmonds regarded the old towpath as "a moving marvel of humanity."[2] But where Adams saw the boaters through the eyes of an essentially romantic novelist and wrote popular fiction with a sentimental and nostalgic flourish for the "good old days," Walter Edmonds's depictions have, more often than not, a more sober ring. Like other major fiction writers who have made use of historical contexts, he grafted an imaginative sensibility upon the facts, in this case the times of canal era America and early York State, to create characters that live in the tragicomedy of real situations.

ROME HAUL

With "admiration, affection, and gratitude," Edmonds dedicated *Rome Haul*, his first novel, to Professor Charles Townsend Copeland of Harvard, who had encouraged the student writer to draw upon the upstate New York memory of his youth. The road from college classroom and Harvard composition course to a first published novel was to prove fairly short and pleasurable. When he applied to Ellery Sedgwick for a job with the *Atlantic Monthly*, Edmonds was persuaded instead, he said, to take a room in Cambridge, to "hole up," and to write a novel about the Erie Canal.[3] Sedgwick also promised to print a manuscript if delivered in four months' time; and Edmonds, at twenty-five, seemed on his way toward becoming a novelist.

"By the first of November," he wrote later in an introduction for the Modern Library edition of the novel which resulted, "I was installed in a room, with a typewriter, and the second morning I wrote 'Rome Haul' at the top of the page, 'I' under it, and under that "The Road and the Peddler.' 'In 1850 the road to Boonville wound out of the Tug Hill country . . .' No fresh start, no hesitation: I finished the first chapter by lunch time. That morning at breakfast I had thought of a peddler describing the Erie, saying of it, 'it's the bowels of the nation, it's the whole shebang of life.' I thought it was good for an opening chapter, and it turned out to be good for the whole book."[4]

The manuscript of the novel which Edmonds had promised for delivery to the *Atlantic* editor in March was completed almost five weeks early. His youthful enthusiasm had produced a book much longer than Sedgwick wanted, and some seventy thousand words had to be excised. They compromised, Edmonds recalled, and so long as the *Atlantic* editors did the pruning, he didn't mind. *Rome Haul* became an Atlantic Monthly Press book for 1929, and both the public and the critics received it warmly. "'Rome Haul,'" commented the reviewer for the *New York Tribune*, "would be a notable book in any season. As the first novel of a man born in 1903 it is extraordinary."[5] And *Rome Haul* was extraordinary for it was a pioneer work. Edmonds had purposefully set out to write a novel set in canal country, pervaded with canal life in all its teeming, bustling aspects, and reflecting the commercial as well as the human image of the canalling days on Clinton's Ditch. The book was a pioneer work, too, in establishing what might reasonably be called a new genre, for it is the first novel to deal in its entirety with the Erie Canal.[6] Its popularity, at any rate, extended to Broadway and motion picture adaptations, and to inclusion in the Modern Library series—impressive achievements for a first novel.

The novel derives essentially from three sources: tales of the old canallers with whom Edmonds had talked during his winters at Boonville; a couple of scrapbooks of newspaper clippings kept by his grandfather in the 1850s and 1860s; and, finally, Alvin Harlow's nostalgic and full treatment of canal days, *Old Towpaths*.[7] The canal that bulks large in *Rome Haul* is the Erie, not the Black River Canal; and the Erie Canal seen in these pages is that of the mid-nineteenth century, a time when the heyday of the sleek packet boats had passed and when passenger trade was more and more being lost to the railroads. Freight hauling was, in 1850, the chief commercial activity on the "canawl"; and Edmonds's novel deals, therefore, with people who earn their livelihood from boating or who are otherwise significantly affected by the great inland waterway. The basic theme of the book is that of finding one's self, of maturing; and in the action the orphan Dan Harrow, coming out of Black River country, rises quickly through numerous opportune circumstances from an initial job as a "hoggee" (canalese for "towpath driver boy"[8]) to become captain of his own boat engaged in traffic on what was referred to as "the Rome haul."

As Edmonds had said, an old peddler sets the tone for the whole novel with his remarks to Dan Harrow at the outset. As Harrow makes his way toward Rome, New York, and an eventual job on the Erie, this peddler, Turnesa, talks to him about the significance of Clinton's Ditch:

View on Erie Canal by J. W. Hill, 1830–32. Photograph from the I. N. Phelps Stokes Collection, Arts, Prints and Photographs Division, The New York Public Library, Astor, Lenox and Tilden Foundations.

. . . The Erie is a swarming hive. Boats, coming and going, passing you all the while. You can hear their horns blowing all day long. As like as not there's a fight at every lock. There's all kind of people there, and they're all going all the while. It ain't got the finish and style as when the packet boats was running, but you'll find fancy folks in the big ports. It's better without the packet boats; let the railroads take the passengers. It leaves the pace steady for growing. There's freight going west and raw food east, all on the canal; there's people going west, New Englanders, Germans, all them furrin folk, and there's people coming east that've quit. But the canawlers keep a-moving.

Water-level trade route, they call it, and it is. By grab, it's the bowels of the nation! It's the whole shebang of life. [P. 8]

This newspaper artist's sketch from an old drawing c. 1840 shows a packet boat entering the lock at Rome, New York. Photograph courtesy of the Utica *Daily Press*.

As one might expect in a book set along a waterway extending some 360 miles—the longest single canal ever built—across New York State, Turnesa's opening remarks about the Erie's being a "swarming hive" are borne out by the plethora of characters Edmonds creates for his novel. This was a characteristic he subsequently followed in other works which have at times seemed, especially to his critics, overpopulated.

Harrow's first contact with the Erie Canal itself and with the boaters recalled to him the last words of the old peddler. The Black River lad found the Erie complex, earthy, veritably "the bowels of the nation" that Turnesa had pronounced it; but it was also awe inspiring and adventurous. The picture Edmonds draws of Dan Harrow's meeting the canal for the first time is Whitmanesque in its romantic yet utilitarian sweep:

> . . . "the whole shebang of life." He could see it in the hurry and a certain breathlessness above the easy noise; he could smell it in the boats coming from the West, the raw foods, the suffocating odor of grain, the scent of meat, of pork, the homely smell of potatoes, to be digested in the East and produce growth. It mystified him, though he seemed to understand it, and it stirred a great affection in him for living, for the people round him, and the clean light of the sun. [P. 57]

The essential interest in humanity, to say nothing of Edmonds's realistic depiction of the melting pot that was early America, is reflected again and again in the opening chapters as Dan Harrow stands and stares, wide eyed and wondering, for all of America and much of Europe seemed to be on the canal.

> . . . The boats, more than he could count, coming in and going out, many passing through without a stop, each with a man steering and a man walking behind a towing team, moving at a slow pace, but giving an impression of an intense, suppressed desire for speed. The line boats, recognizable for the hard faces of their captains, largely Irishers, brought in gangs when the great work of the canal was coming to a close; they had an air about them of men aware of physical well-being. Boats bearing emigrants out to the West, Germans, an old man on one with a mug in his hand and a long china pipe to his mouth and a nightcap on his head, stiffly promenading the deck in his stocking feet; and tow-haired children on another. A New Englander going by, driving a boat, a cold-faced bearded man who spoke in a nasal tight voice ordinary words to his horses more impressive than oaths; a boy steering, his young face grimly serious. Two boats of tall, light-haired folk,—"Hunkers" said a man at Dan's back . . .—but they had a light in their blue eyes.
> Boats of all colors—greys, greens, blues, reds, muddy magentas, and many white, floating on their reflections, many bearing strange folk, entering a strange country . . . [P. 50]

These immigrants, "entering a strange country" symbolize

Dan Harrow's own entry into an alien life on the canal, one away from the farmland of his birth.

The story line of *Rome Haul* is relatively straightforward, like a popular romance; but the depth to which Edmonds probes his characters and recaptures the spirit of the times when canalling was a necessary part of things are praiseworthy accomplishments. Dan Harrow, starting out as a hoggee, comes into possession of a canal boat, the *Sarsey Sal*, that was owned originally by a captain who had known Dan's father and who died of the cholera in one of those epidemics which caused much anguish in early nineteenth-century New York. Molly Larkins, taken on as cook, is the girl who provides a romantic incentive to Dan and who serves as an impetus to his maturing. Molly's having left Jotham Klore, a husky canaller of the brag-and-fight school, helps set the stage for a series of crises, both romantic and psychological, that make Dan Harrow's career as a canaller one of tension and conflict. The love that develops between Dan Harrow and Molly Larkin adds romantic charm and also intensifies the conflict he faces in weighing the life of a boater against the call of farming.

The desirability of marrying Molly, making their relationship legal rather than "just a working agreement" (which often was the case on the canal), proves troublesome to Dan, who faces the problem of losing her if he turns his back on Erie water and a canalling life:

> "You can ask her," said Mrs. Gurget, "but I don't think it would help. And if you ask her, it's like saying—"the fat woman shied clear of her words. "Mostly there ain't anything wrong in not being married on the canal. As long as you're honest there ain't any real sense in it. It's different if you're going to get off the canal. Then you've got to act like other folks. But here living's just a working agreement, and if you want you can get a minister to lick the revenue stamp to seal it with; but it don't add a lot. And a gal's free to back out. Sometimes it makes it hard for her, but if she wants it that way, it ain't any bother of yours. Unless you want to take her off'n the canal. Be you going to stick at boating, Dan?" [P. 253]

The novel is unified around three principal conflicts, the first of which is the boy-girl conflict of Dan versus Molly. A second conflict, one that develops inevitably from the first, is that of Dan Harrow versus Klore. The third, a background conflict which affects in varying ways all the characters, is that of the canal versus the railroad, for more and more in this period of New York State history, the heyday of canalism was waning, giving ground to the economic and technological efficiency of steam.

Molly Larkins is, seemingly, the catalyst in Dan Harrow's maturing in *Rome Haul;* but when he has matured he loses her. The outcome of the struggle between Jotham Klore and Dan over Molly —a fight that had long been brewing with considerable apprehensiveness on the part of the basically shy and nonbelligerent Harrow —is a victory for Dan in that he does best Klore; but in winning the fight he decides to leave the canal for a farming position, and in so doing he loses the girl. Fortune Friendly, the novel's renegade minister who appropriately lives up to his surname, summarizes the situation between the two men with characteristic Yorker terseness: "'It don't seem right,' Fortune said to the rumps of the horses. 'Each one thought he was fighting for her. And neither one won'" (p. 331).

Published at the end of the 1920s, *Rome Haul* contains interesting similarities to works of other writers of the period. To begin with, Edmonds's novel reflects certain characteristic "Lost Generation" themes and style. In several respects, for example, one may regard *Rome Haul* as a kind of "Waste Land" era product, set in regional New York canal country. Certainly, whatever else might be said about it, validly or coincidentally the sense of T. S. Eliot's "HURRY UP PLEASE ITS TIME" pervades the book—in the encroachment of the railroads on the canaller's life with the result of lessening their chances for livelihood; in Dan Harrow's fear of meeting with Jotham Klore for the inevitable showdown; in Molly's uncertainty about and fear of marriage; and in the highwayman Gentleman Joe Calash's vain search for freedom from the pursuit by his "mantrackers." In Dan Harrow's identification with the soil—his name is an obvious symbol—that keeps calling him back to the upstate dairy country and "off'n the canal," there is also this same urgency. Yet, like John Dos Passos's Jimmy Herf and F. Scott Fitzgerald's Amory Blaine, Dan's heading into farmlands beyond the Erie Canal may signify a positive upturn, an "escape" to better things. Even more confidently than they, Dan Harrow faces his future, once his decision is made, with an affirmation: "and he thought of the fine cattle he was to work among," Edmonds says at the close of the novel; "already he was looking forward." For him, the canal was just a way station on the road to maturity.[9]

Edmonds's novel is, of course, important as a work of literature not merely because it may share similar characteristics with
other fiction of the well-known writers of the twenties, or necessarily
because it reflects that period's literary and cultural currents. First
and foremost, *Rome Haul* is a regional novel in the best sense, opening the way—one is tempted to say "the sluice gates"—for a surprisingly large number of novels dealing with this region of the United
States.[10] In particular, his work proved to be an influence on other
authors to find themes, characters, and settings for stories and novels that have resulted in a considerable canal literature. *Rome Haul*
established—with its canal bully, its canal argot, its climactic hero-
versus-bully fistfight—what have become conventions of the canal
novel; for these fictional conventions have been followed by other
writers dealing with the Erie Canal and its boaters. Edmonds's
novel not only captured the brawling and buoyant spirit of a past era
in American history but also, most importantly, presented basic human issues in a way that transcends any narrow regionalism. The
universal conflicts of maturing, of love, of struggle against an adversary, are all there. In *Rome Haul* Edmonds thus created a novel
deeper in significance than an entertaining story, though the novel is
assuredly that as well.

CANALLERS ON BROADWAY

There can be little doubt about the popularity of *Rome Haul.* The
original edition was reprinted three times in 1929, its first year; and
three other printings came from Little, Brown between 129 and
1938. In that same year, 1938, the novel was added to the Modern Library series which Random House was developing. The book became
a popular play when adapted for the stage in the 1930s, as well
as a motion picture that starred Janet Gaynor and Henry Fonda.
Twentieth-Century Fox did a technicolor remake of the movie version in 1952, with a considerably altered script, which saw Betty
Grable and Dale Robertson in the leading roles of Molly and Dan
Harrow. In the spring of 1962, Edmonds's original novel, *Rome
Haul,* was reissued (along with *Drums along the Mohawk* and *Erie
Water*) under the collective title *Three Stalwarts.*
    Rome Haul was first dramatized by Frank B. Elser as *Low*

Bridge, a three-act romantic comedy which had its premiere in the fall of 1932 under a program whereby a group of university and community theater directors sponsored simultaneous openings of new plays outside of New York.[11] *Low Bridge* actually had two "world premieres" as a result. It was produced at Northwestern University on October 18, 19, and 20, 1932. "World Premiere Wins Praise of Many Critics" ran a headline above an article in the *Daily Northwestern* describing the presentation, which was directed by John P. Baird, with Rhett Milligen and Robert Breen playing the parts of the boater's cook and the "country boy with high ideals."[12] The play was also produced at the University of Iowa, with Vance M. Morton as the director, and Mary P. Bennett and Richard H. Anderson cast as Molly and Dan. It opened at Iowa on October 21, 1932, at a special Homecoming performance the weekend before the regular theater season began.[13] Among those present were Daniel Frohman, longtime dean of American theatrical managers, and Frank Elser, the author of the play. Elser was a newspaperman who worked "in and around New York," had been a war correspondent for the Associated Press in 1914 and 1915 in Europe, and covered the Villa campaign in Mexico with General Pershing for the *New York Times,* where he was also night city editor. An earlier play of his, *Mr. Gilhooley,* produced in New York by Jed Harris, starred Arthur Sinclair of the Abbey Theatre, along with actress Helen Hayes.

Low Bridge was the season's first play at both locations and the first of the series to go to Broadway. When Elser's attempts at reworking the play himself proved unsatisfactory, he consulted Marc Connelly, whose recognition as a dramatist began with *Dulcy* (1921) and *Merton of the Movies* (1922), both written in collaboration with George S. Kaufman, and whose Pulitzer Prize play *The Green Pastures* (1930) made important use of folk, if not regional, idiom. The Elser-Connelly collaboration resulted, finally, in a successful drama out of *Rome Haul.* They called it *The Farmer Takes a Wife.*

Cast and directed by Connelly and produced by Max Gordon, the play had a pre-Broadway opening in Washington, D.C. June Walker, who had the part of Molly, had suggested for her leading man a fellow named Henry Fonda who had a role with her husband, Geoffrey Kerr, in *The Swan.* "We opened on Monday night," Fonda said, "and Tuesday morning we woke up to top-notch reviews."[14] As a result Max Gordon offered Fonda his first run-of-the-play contract, the first time the young actor had tenure for the duration of a play, as well as the best salary—$225 a week—he had made so far. *Farmer*

Scene from the Fox Film *The Farmer Takes a Wife* showing the *Sarsey Sal* on a romanticized Erie Canal in 1850. This motion picture, based on Walter D. Edmonds's highly successful first novel, *Rome Haul,* starred Janet Gaynor and Henry Fonda. Photograph courtesy of Twentieth Century-Fox,

A canal boat approaches a lock and "locks through" in this scene from the motion picture *The Farmer Takes a Wife.* The setting and time is typical of other Walter D. Edmonds's novels such as *Erie Water* and *The Wedding*

opened in New York's Forty-Sixth Street Theater on October 30, 1934, for a run of one hundred and four performances. "New York turned out to be better than Washington," Fonda's biographer noted. "Applause for June Walker. Acclamation for Henry Fonda."[15]

When the play tried out in Boston, Connelly recruited Ed-

Journey. Photographs courtesy of Twentieth Century-Fox, copyright ©
1935 Twentieth Century-Fox Film Corp. All rights reserved.

monds to provide the horses. "Putting on the play was great fun,"
Edmonds said. "Marc gave me the assignment of finding stage
horses here in Boston (where the play did not draw enough people to
pay the lighting bill) and in New York. My only other contribution
was to write the few lines spoken by Fonda and the blacksmith in the

Horse-drawn canal boats on the Erie Canal in Rome, New York, as depicted in the motion picture *The Farmer Takes a Wife*. Photograph courtesy of Twentieth Century-Fox, copyright © 1935 Twentieth Century-Fox Film Corp. All rights reserved.

coming of dawn scene under the canal towpath. It was a nice cozy sort of play."[16] A program note for the production provides a sense of the play's purpose as scripted by the playwrights:

> America today has almost forgotten 'The Grand Canawl,' which was the Erie. For more than a century it surpassed all other agencies in feeding our growing nation with men and supplies from

Charles Bickford and Janet Gaynor in a scene with the *Sarsey Sal,* the canal boat featured in *The Farmer Takes a Wife,* a Fox Film based on the Marc Connelly play and Walter D. Edmonds's novel *Rome Haul.* Photograph courtesy of Twentieth Century-Fox, copyright © 1935 Twentieth Century-Fox Film Corp. All rights reserved.

the Atlantic seaboard. Opened in 1825, it ran its slow but teeming course, more than 350 miles, between Albany and Buffalo, not only bringing wealth and expansion to the villages in its path, but hastening incalculably the development of the pioneer West. *The Farmer Takes a Wife* attempts to recapture some of the simple excitements of the people of that vanished era.[17]

An interior scene on the canal boat *Sarsey Sal* from the motion picture *The Farmer Takes a Wife* depicts 1850 period furnishings. Janet Gaynor, as Molly Larkins, starred with Henry Fonda in this motion picture based on Walter D. Edmonds's *Rome Haul.* Photograph courtesy of Twentieth Century-Fox, copyright © 1935 Twentieth Century-Fox Film Corp. All rights reserved.

Burns Mantle chose the play as one of the year's ten best for his annual anthology of Broadway dramas,[18] but the subsequent stage history of *The Farmer Takes a Wife* has not been notable. Edmonds's world in *Rome Haul*, the novel, is an essentially and fully dramatic one, but the drama of a historical context which sees ordinary people confront the problem of changing times does not always make good theater. In reviewing the Broadway production of *The Farmer Takes a Wife*, the periodical *Theatre Arts Monthly* suggested that the simple excitements of that life were perhaps *too* simple to re-create. "Whatever it is," their reviewer stated, "the play lacks impulse, and the audience accepts without a fight the fact that in a year or two after the play's time the Erie Canal will be only a ditch and not worth their bothering about." While the writer's critical, theaterwise comment may have been on target, his knowledge of history was not altogether accurate, for the canal did not fade as abruptly as he indicated; at any rate, he said, "these far-away plays" were needed "as a background for the mass of plays based on our quick, modern living."[19] The reviewer suggested, in conclusion, that a repertory theater might be a better home for *The Farmer Takes a Wife*; there it "might round out its players and its playing and find a happy niche."

That was good advice, and one post-Broadway production, by the Charles Coburn Mohawk Drama Festival on the grounds of Union College, apparently took it. Coburn's production in the summer of 1937 came close to the original novel in geographic setting by utilizing a natural outdoor stage and the atmosphere of a former canal town: "Old Dorp" (Schenectady, New York), which provides a locale now and then in Edmonds's fiction—fifteen miles as the crow flies from Albany, the state capital on the Hudson River but twenty-seven tedious locks away by canal boat in the nineteenth century over the Cohoes Falls.

The theatrical side of the *Rome Haul* story, especially since the book was Edmonds' first novel, is of critical interest. To compare Edmonds's novel with the Frank Elser play, *Low Bridge* and the collaborative Elser-Connelly *The Farmer Takes a Wife* leads to highly interesting conclusions for the critic of literature. While all three works are overtly related, *Low Bridge* is largely a colloquial piece; *The Farmer Takes a Wife* is a successful albeit by no means outstanding romantic comedy; and *Rome Haul*, the original novel, is actually much more the drama.[20] In both stage adaptations the fight climax occurs as in the novel but with less dramatic intensity; and in the plays the romantic artificialities prevail as the boy-meets-girl theme is brought to its expected and conventional resolution with love triumphing. (Molly's going out to meet Dan and leaving the canal forms an appropriately romantic if conventional conclusion to the motion picture version as well.) In the novel Molly leaves Dan; and, in doing so, frees him, as it were, to return to farming. In *Rome Haul,* therefore, the novelist has achieved what the dramatists and scriptwriters following him either could not do or did not care to do; for Edmonds's handling of the situation at the close of his novel depicts a maturity which accepts life as it is (and was) in the canal era, with its ups and downs, its losses and its promises.

CANALLERS AND FARMERS: *THE BIG BARN*

For his second published novel, *The Big Barn* (1930), Edmonds turned his full attention to the Black River farmlands that he knew during his boyhood. Howard Thomas tells us in his *Black River in the North Country* that Edmonds's novel is a fictionalized account of the building of a barn on the Lyon estate near High Falls, north of Boonville.[21] Dan Harrow from Edmonds's first book appears again as a character in this one; and, momentarily at least, the old peddler Turnesa, also from *Rome Haul,* puts in an appearance. Yet this second novel gives Dan Harrow, who figured so prominently in the first, only a minor role to play; and the canal (the Black River Canal, this time, which came down from the North Country to join the Erie at Rome, New York) serves merely as background as the author, in filling out the characterizations of some of his cast, mentions their having worked on the canal or having served as canal commissioners. The story line of this novel concerns Ralph Wilder, a patriarch of the upcountry Tug Hill area whom Edmonds describes as "a handsome old desperado" and as an old man who "loved his possessions" (pp. 93, 129); his son Bascom, who felt his life tied to the tradition of farming; and his one grand project—the big barn:

> "Some say I'm crazy to build such a barn," he told his daughter-in-law.
> "They say it's too big, but I came here when this side of the river was all woods and every inch of this land cleared and splendid

crops come on to it. The land needs cattle, and they need the barn. If it's too big I'll get more farm land. When a man like me gets older, girl, he doesn't care for people. I'm not afraid to die, but I've got to do something. And that barn will stand a while." [P. 76]

The Big Barn is thus not a canal novel, and it stands somewhat anachronistically between Edmonds's two major novels about the canal, *Rome Haul* and *Erie Water* (1933). Robert M. Gay, writing in the *Atlantic Monthly*, called it "an extended character study" in discussing Edmonds's work[22]; and certainly Edmonds's portrait of old Ralph Wilder is one. Ralph Wilder had been one of the commissioners charged with digging the canal, and he had constructed the first river steamer; he had built a house for his wife better than any other in the North Country; he had served in the State Assembly; and he had created a kind of dynasty for himself out of the wilderness area where he and his father settled. Yet, the novel is both Wilder's and not Wilder's, for the plot revolves so closely around his daughter-in-law, his son Henry's wife Rose, that she emerges as far and away the central figure of the book. She moves those with whom she comes into contact and is moved by them; therefore, she is a literary sister to Daphne DuMaurier's Melanie in *Rebecca* who has more than a catalyst's role to play in the action of the story. The allusion is not inappropriate, for something of the "second wife status" is felt as Rose Wilder, a Boston girl seemingly ill-equipped to be mistress of a York State farm, confronts, in turn, her father-in-law, the farm's housekeeper Mrs. Brinley, and finally her own destinies.

Rose Wilder is the temporal strength of the novel; Ralph Wilder is the endurance of it. Rose reacts almost immediately upon her introduction to the family to Bascom's rakish attractiveness; at the same time she sets out to establish herself as full mistress of the household. She desired this necessary "sense of establishment," and she succeeds in gaining it: "She saw very clearly one thing. She had made herself a place where people looked to her as she liked to have them" (p. 175). All "look to her" that is, except her husband Henry, the son who preferred Latin to farming and who, like Charles Bovary in Flaubert's novel, thought too little of his wife's real needs for love. Rose Wilder has something of William Dean Howells's Editha in her make-up, but without Editha's moral shallowness; she also has something of Flaubert's Emma Bovary in that make-up, but without Emma's callous disregard for the practical. "She might give it," Edmonds tells us, in regard to her almost overwhelming desire to have an affair with her brother-in-law Bascom, "if it were not for a streak of practical hard sense that said, 'Is it worth while?'" (p. 185). In some ways with Rose Wilder's strength and commonsense Edmonds seems to be saying that she, Boston background and all, was an upstate New Yorker, that she "belonged" more than even old Ralph gave her credit for.

In this novel about the 1860s Edmonds's style retained the element of natural at-homeness that he had used in *Rome Haul* and in numerous short stories, with their sketches of canallers and scenes of York State countryside; but the relative paucity of characters and the generally static locale contrasts sharply with the more heavily populated plot and broader canvas of the earlier *Rome Haul* and of later novels like *Erie Water* and *Drums Along the Mohawk*, all of which have dozens of characters, shifting locales, and subplots. In *The Big Barn* the author focused upon events in the lives of members of one family; this delineation of one household and the central theme of endurance, represented by Ralph Wilder and symbolized by the barn, has a definite Faulkner-like ring to it. Actually, it was several years after the publication of Edmonds's *The Big Barn* that William Faulkner depicted his "grand design" of Thomas Sutpen in *Absalom, Absalom!* (1936). In his novel of 1930 Edmonds presented his portrayal of the formation of a dynasty in an American hinterland: the house Ralph Wilder built

> had no counterpart north of the Mohawk Valley. Sixty thousand dollars had gone into it. The stone had been quarried seven miles away in Collinsville across the river. He had hired an architect to build it in a French style, and after his last term in the Assembly they had come back to live here. [Pp. 4–5]
>
> More than forty years before he had come into the valley with his father, who had been land agent for the Courtney Purchase. Little by little, first together, then he alone, they had bought up timberland, until now he owned a hundred thousand acres of the finest timber stretching from his farm south and eastward up the rivers. He held mortgages on half the farms along the valley, ten miles in each direction; he owned the water power on the creeks and the great red mill beside the falls. Of plain Scotch and English stock, he and his father had come into this valley and by a grim and ruthless sort of industry had made it theirs. [P. 4]

When the barn was completed, that too was Ralph Wilder's: "The old man looked about him. The barn was done. Above his head hung the net of beams, the completed web—all his; every stick of it out of his own woods. Only the shingles came from southward, but they had come by the canal that he had helped to build" [p. 76]. Endurance and tradition are, for Edmonds as for Faulkner, the twin values of one' inheritance. From these values, not always without human tarnishing to be sure, American civilization has been forged. Ralph Wilder and his big barn are Edmonds's testimonial to the endurance and tradition of the North Country folk of upstate New York.

BUILDING THE GRAND CANAL: *ERIE WATER*

If Edmonds's depiction of the canal life into which the young hero of *Rome Haul* is immersed seems Whitman-like, certainly in *Erie Water* (1933), his third published novel, the Erie Canal itself becomes a symbol of technological progress and of democratic achievement even more akin to the Whitmanesque. Like Walt Whitman's locomotive, Walter D. Edmonds's canal is seen as a "type of the modern"; it was wrought by hands and minds largely unskilled in engineering, but the creators were imbued with a Yorker initiative, shrewdness, and common sense. Where *Rome Haul* dealt with the canal at the middle of the century, with its heyday actually passing, *Erie Water* unfolds the romantic story of the building of the Big Ditch. It spans the period of the initial construction of the Old Erie, that is, from 1817 to the completion in 1825. Two volumes of the laws of the State of New York, in particular, "formed the bones of my description of digging and building locks," Edmonds said. He found these and other material for *Erie Water* in the Hamilton College Library at Clinton, New York, not far from the towpath town of Utica. There the librarian, Mr. Ibbotson, he recalled appreciatively, "very kindly let me have a desk in a window and the run of the stacks."[23]

The principal characters in *Erie Water* are, just as in his first novel, two young persons: Jerry Fowler, a Lebanon Valley youth of twenty-two, who is determined to make his own way in the world; and Mary Goodhill, an English redemptioner whose papers of indenture Fowler buys at the outset as he passes through Albany, New York, on his trek to the western territory. The love that develops between Jerry Fowler and Mary Goodhill, and the domestic crises brought about by Jerry's having to travel far from her side as he becomes heavily involved in canal contracting provide the basic romantic plot of the novel. But Jerry Fowler, like Dan Harrow in *Rome Haul,* has some growing up to do. In a real sense he matures as the Erie Canal nears completion: Jerry Fowler comes of age only when water from Lake Erie finally flows over the canal to the Hudson River at its eastern terminus.

The story's plot and setting both are thus closely canal connected. Fowler is hired in Utica by a canal contractor, Caleb Hammil, to help build the first locks on the canal. Typical of the pioneering contractors, Hammil didn't even know what a canal lock looked like when he won the $17,000 contract for laying foundations for the Erie locks and aqueducts. With Yorker good humor and common sense he turned aside a query about the locks. "Well," he said, "I'm a contractor and no mechanic. I've never seen one. But they've got them down in Massachusetts, so I guess we can build them. Anyway, I've got a book about it" (p. 108).

Through such characters *Erie Water* traces the story of the building of Clinton's Ditch, from the initial spadeful of earth turned at Rome, New York, in 1817, to the completion of the job with the famous paired double-lock "combines" at Lockport. Edmonds's hero, young Fowler, is drawn into that final activity, too: "You and I started the first lock," the engineer Nathan Roberts told him. "In 1817—six years ago. . . . It would be fun to build the last on the line" (p. 424).

Edmonds divided *Erie Water* into four sections: "The Wedding," "Mary," "Norah," and "Erie Water." Chapter headings are drawn from fragments of dialogue or from lines within the respective parts of the novel, a technique he was to develop even more fully in *Drums Along the Mohawk* several years later. The first three sections of *Erie Water* are each followed by an interlude section of vignettes dealing with the times, which are generally but not always importantly tied in with the principal plot. It was a technique employed with considerable success by William Faulkner in his later Yoknapatawpha novels.

The strength of Edmonds's *Erie Water* lies in his honest depiction of the folkways of the people in a culturally significant era of United States history: the "ether plant" used to soothe an aching tooth; the conversation in Philetus Bumpus' general store when one of the ladies is buying a few yards of calico; the buying and christening of a fine new horse, aptly named "Bourbon"; the hard life in the diggers' shanties and the opportunism possible for those who later buy the buildings after the canal project is completed; and a man's reaction to the whole business of contracting—"Afore this damned canal a man just said he'd work," was Self Rogers's comment. "Now he signs a paper" (p. 168).

The strength of the novel also lies in Edmonds's treatment of the plethora of problems, many of them monumental in those days when the whole profession of engineering was yet to be born: building locks without plans; running a canal bed on an aqueduct over a river like the Genesee, or carving it out of bedrock around a mountain; fighting the malarial fever of the swamps; and overcoming the myriad difficulties of a hostile environment for the sake of economic progress. He does in prose what Philip Freneau memorialized in poetry as "a work from Nature's chaos won."[24] The author makes the reader realize not only the extent of the problems, but he manages also to convey a sense of the intense if unsophisticated jubilance that came with being a part of such pioneering achievement:

> "Let's try the gates!"
> Cosmo Turbe yelled and ran across the beams, his nailed heels leaving marks at every step. They manned the gates together, eight men, six wondering how they worked while Caleb explained to them.
> "She's at the high level for a boat from Rome." His stout voice bellowed. "There comes the mules. Stand back, you dumb bezabor. Do you want to get kicked by a hinny mule?" A tall man ducked aside, so vivid was the sudden picture. Plute guffawed, and clapped his hand upon his mouth. "Whoa!" shouted Hammil, red cheeks all a-sweat. "Easy on that boat there. Do you want to knock her bow in? Here she comes. Right in. Sixty feet of her, loaded to draw three feet with Devereaux whiskey bound for O-hio. Now we close the upper gates. You work that one, Cosmo. The water's at high level. Open up the sluice-leaves in the lower." They ran in two groups down along the lock walls. Only the mason continued sitting on his stone. He had laid up walls that wouldn't come down like Jericho's. Hammil cranked the sluice-leaf open on his side. "The water's running out. You can hear the overflow from east commence upon the tumble bay. The boat's going down. See her! She's eight foot, ten foot, lower than she was. There she is at bottom level. Push round that beam, there, Cosmo!" The lower gates swung open. "Git, you hinny! Git, you mules! There she's easing out. See her. She's bound for Buffalo. Maybe the boater passes me a quart drawn from a keg in fair exchange for water."

With staring eyes the men followed his pointing finger along
the black muck track the grubbers left. They saw the marsh, and
the shadow of a cloud slowly moving.
Suddenly Caleb laughed and tossed his hands apart.
"By gravy, boys! We've finished Number One!" [Pp. 207–208]

Epical as the theme of the building of the famous Big Ditch
was in the history of the state and of the nation, that accomplishment does not necessarily make a unifying force as literarily significant as one might suspect; for Edmonds's novel rambles, and too
many characters, with the exception of the principal cast, appear so
fleetingly they cannot serve purposefully valid literary roles in a recreated past. In their transient appearances even famous historic
personages such as DeWitt Clinton, Benjamin Wright, Myron Hol-
ley, Jemima Wilkinson, and Joseph Smith move as in a kaleidoscope;
to some readers who feel they stumble upon them rather than meeting and knowing them, such characters may well serve more to de-
tract from the overall story than to support it.

Perhaps the Erie Canal background is so obviously the moti-
vating influence that its force in the novel overshadows the characters and the human drama when it appears. *Erie Water* was so historically accurate, Edmonds said, "that it is a wonder anyone ever read
it as a novel."[25] Though it is hard to fault a book because of its historical accuracy, it is possible that the documentary and the created aspects are in conflict. Later, in *Drums Along the Mohawk*, Edmonds
corrected any such deficiency; in that novel, discussed in the next
chapter, the broad canvas required by the circumstances of the
American Revolution could be peopled with both unknown and
known characters of a real past in a way which successfully moved
the novel beyond mere historical romance toward the plateau of art.

As his second canal novel Edmonds's *Erie Water* suggests
comparison with the earlier *Rome Haul*. Where Molly Larkins and
Dan Harrow in Edmonds's first novel have spirit and honest desires,
Jerry Fowler and his young wife move somewhat less thinkingly.
Events move and make Fowler: he does not even meditate seriously
upon them as Dan Harrow does. Worse still is Mary, who mopes
through the novel hardly rippling the surface of life; she is so re-
signed to events that the reader may be surprised when, finally, she
musters an uncharacteristic gumption and allows herself to be taken
off by a wandering cobbler. Note that neither Dan nor Jerry keeps
his woman. There are other, if minor, parallels, deliberate or coinci-

dental, between the two works. Issachar Bennet, a "Shaker Missioner," corresponds rather easily to Fortune Friendly in *Rome Haul;* both might be described as renegade ministers preaching a pragmatic humanism while retaining some semblance of attachment to the cloth. Henry Falk, the itinerant cobbler, moves across the landscape in almost the same way—with the same sense of nefarious purpose, as far as the reader knows—as the renegade Joe Calash does in the earlier novel. Dan Harrow's fight with Jotham Klore, which provides the climactic event in *Rome Haul,* finds at least a weak parallel in the brawl between O'Mory and Jay-Jay in the closing pages of *Erie Water.* In both books the canal is, of course, the essential theme —if not, perhaps, the real hero.

Whatever its faults, *Erie Water* should not be dismissed as a less effective copy of *Rome Haul.* "Mr. Edmonds' narrative," said one contemporary reviewer, "is much like the canal itself, placid, even, unhurried, taking the reader on a lengthy journey, which, almost surprisingly, does not grow monotonous but proves to develop something interesting all along the way."[26] *Erie Water* does have much to offer the reader, and it will not disappoint even today's television-reared browser who picks up a library copy. The novel is validly interesting on its own terms: a depiction of the beginning of the canal days in America and of the historic building of New York's grand Erie Canal.

5

Drums Along the Mohawk

I HAVE JUST FINISHED WRITING A NOVEL about the Mohawk Valley during the Revolutionary War and I feel a little as if I had caught a big fish," said Edmonds in an *Atlantic Monthly* article a month after *Drums Along the Mohawk* came out.[1] In July 1936, Little, Brown and Company had published his novel of nearly five hundred pages dealing with Mohawk Valley settlers facing the events of 1775 and 1776. Over the preceding few months parts of the novel had been appearing as stories in the *Saturday Evening Post.* The initial print order of ten thousand copies[2] gave no suggestion that *Drums Along the Mohawk,* Walter D. Edmonds's fifth book and fourth published novel, was to become a bestseller of more than half a million copies. Nor did the reviews, while very few were unfavorable, indicate that a twentieth-century classic had been written. Edmonds had, after all, written other novels that could be considered historical novels, and the first, *Rome Haul,* had even made the "Hollywood connection"; in addition, these earlier works had been quite successful with the public, though perhaps not to an extent that placed their author's name in every critic's column. Many of the reviewers of *Drums Along the Mohawk* failed to recognize the essential epical quality of Edmonds's latest book when it appeared. *Atlantic* editor Edward Weeks, who had succeeded Sedgwick, considered it a good story but saw "no epic grandeur," and historian Allan Nevins, reviewing the book for the *Saturday Review of Literature,* merely continued the already established position of praising Edmonds as a novelist who "very well paints a society, a countryside full of people."[3]

But Edmonds was right: he had caught a big fish. *Drums Along the Mohawk* made Edmonds's reputation among later critics, most of whom today would agree with one editor's observation that the book represents "one of the best examples of the regional chronicle ever written in America."[4] The Book-of-the-Month Club helped establish Walter D. Edmonds in the eyes of the general reading public: the book became an August selection in the year it was published. Only Margaret Mitchell's blockbuster (as it turned out to be) *Gone With the Wind*, which came out at the same time, kept Edmonds's new novel from the top of the bestseller list. Even so, he did not fare badly. "Book of the Month Club had decided on my book when the Mitchell manuscript came in," he explained in a 1976 interview. "So they ended up with two historical novels. And for one week, 'Drums' was number one on the Best Seller List, ahead of 'Gone With the Wind.' But then it was number two after that."[5] Edmonds's novel has been continuously in print since its original appearance. More than fifty-five Little, Brown editions have been sold. Reprint paperback editions in 1950 and 1957 sold more than three hundred and ten thousand copies, with second and third printings totaling an additional sixty-eight thousand copies in the early 1960s. The Bantam Pathfinder edition, first published in February 1963, sold nearly twenty thousand copies in roughly the first year.[6] Book club and other reprint editions add to the total. *Drums Along the Mohawk* was also included, along with *Rome Haul* and *Erie Water*, in the collected three-novel volume, *Three Stalwarts,* which Little, Brown issued in 1962. That, too, is still in print.

THE NOVEL

In *Drums Along the Mohawk,* Walter D. Edmonds wrote about the Mohawk Valley farmers as they faced the coming of the Revolutionary War, and as they endured and survived it. The focus of the novel is essentially their story—a story about ordinary people leading, or trying to lead, ordinary lives in pioneer, frontier America. The theme is not so much patriotism as endurance, not so much love between boy and girl as the need to love, and not so much the generals and officials whose actions are recorded in the history textbooks as the activities of the militiamen and scouts who were the daily makers of history. The theme is epical, not because a war has been fought and won, but because the participants in that war have, as Edmonds himself expressed it in a prefatory note, "laid the foundations of a great and lasting community." Regionalism has become in the pages of this book a vehicle for depicting moving, human drama.

The events covered in the novel span the time period from 1776 to 1781, with an epilogue chapter briefly describing resettlement life in 1784, when the Mohawk Valley had returned to peace within the hard-won context of a United States of America. That final chapter is Lana Martin's, one of those who endured and survived. "We've got this place," she says in the last passage in the novel. "We've got the children. We've got each other. Nobody can take those things away. Not any more" (p. 592).

The Mohawk Valley was a wise choice for the setting of a novel of the American Revolution, quite apart from the fact of the Boonville-born author's first-hand knowledge of the area. The first significant battle of the conflict was fought, and won, at Oriskany, and the final battle was won by New York's militiamen against a retreating John Butler while news of Washington's defeat of Cornwallis at Yorktown was being delivered upstate. The eastern and central New York State area was the scene of the major action of the British and Indian marauders—the "destructives," as they are referred to—and their final routing became the critical factor in the settlers' practical realization of the "life, liberty, and pursuit of happiness" that Thomas Jefferson had spelled out in eloquent Lockean terms in the Declaration of Independence.

To the York State farmer of 1776, however, the rhetorical eloquence of statesmen, the actions of the Continental Congress, and the larger strategies of a centralized military command had a faraway aspect. For the first long years of the struggle for American independence, he hardly realized—and had little time to ponder—the implications beyond the region where he lived:

> ... The plain farmer, thinking of his hay and wheat, had no real idea of what the war was about. In the evenings, reverting to the subject listlessly, all he recalled was the early days of 1775, when the Butlers and the Johnsons and their sheriff, Alexander White, had ridden the length of the valley to chop down the liberty pole in front of Herkimer Church, as they had done at Caughanawaga. But now they were all skyhooted off to Canada for these two years.
>
> It seemed they couldn't take account of the messengers riding

horseback up and down the Kingsroad. Men who went at a gallop
and didn't stop to drink. All they thought of was that you couldn't
find day labor any more for love or money. [P. 168]

Edmonds begins his story just as the marriage of Gilbert
Martin and Magdelana Borst concludes in the Palatine Church at
Fox's Mills. It was a simple ceremony. The wedding was attended by
the bride's family; the Domine, the Reverend Daniel Gros, and his
wife; and "a couple of Indians, half drunk, who had heard of the ceremony and happened over from Indian Castle in hopes of getting invited to the breakfast." The time is July 1776, and the members of
the wedding party are impressed by the Domine's having written in
the family Bible that the marriage had been performed in "Tryon
County, State of New York." Gilbert Martin in this year of independence took his bride Lana to a wilderness settlement—almost the
limits of civilization—where he introduced her to the land he owned,
free and clear. There they lived in a small cabin he had put up himself
the year before, with a muddy brook nearby, a decent pasture area
for the cow they brought with them, two acres of adjoining swamp
grass, and seemingly endless wilderness beyond.

The Martins' trip via the Kingsroad through the Mohawk
Valley, past the Eldridge settlement opposite the German Flats, the
settlement at West Canada Creek crossing, through Schuyler, Cos-
by's Manor, and finally to the Deerfield Settlement, its westernmost
well-traveled limits, was an easy depiction for Edmonds, whose Erie
Canal in *Rome Haul* and *Erie Water* followed in its eastern section
much the same route. West of Deerfield lay the Oriskany Creek Indian camp and Fort Stanwix (later Rome, New York), in 1776 a fort
sadly in need of repair. Against such a backdrop real human beings
once lived and worked; in *Drums Along the Mohawk* the re-creation
is sound, the characters credible, their lives depicted with honesty
and simplicity. The drama of *Drums Along the Mohawk* is a very human one, as it is enacted against the Mohawk background; in Deerfield; in Fort Dayton, to which the settlers fell back as the war pro-
gressed; at Mrs. McKlennar's farmhouse; with the Tory John Wolff
in his Newgate Prison; or at other locales in upstate New York in this
Revolutionary War era.

The plan of the novel resembles, in outline, documentary history. Except for an initial chapter and a closing one devoted to the
Martins, and one chapter given over to the escape of the Tory sympa-
thizer Wolff from prison (Chapter 5), the sections of the book de-

scribe the major sites of action within the Mohawk Valley: "Deerfield: 1776," "Oriskany: 1777," "Stanwix: 1777," "German Flats: 1777–1778," "Onondaga: 1779," "McKlennar's: 1780," and "West Canada Creek: 1781." Edmonds researched his background material with the historian's instincts and thoroughness. "Before I was well embarked on the writing of the book," said Edmonds, "I knew when the snow was falling, and how deep it was; how high the river came, and when there was rain."[7]

The *Atlantic* editor, Edward Weeks, recalled that Walter originally had called his story *A Starving Wilderness,* which, he said, "was not exactly an inviting title for the Depression." Weeks tells how he discussed it with another Boston publisher, Alfred R. McIntyre, who had, Weeks admitted, a most astonishing grasp of detail:

> ... We were struggling together for the right title for a new novel by Walter Edmonds, a novel describing the fortitude and misery of the colonists in the Mohawk Valley at the time of the American Revolution.
> Alfred, as he fingered the manuscript, said, "These people lived in the Mohawk Valley. 'Mohawk' is a good word." Pause. "How did the news of the Revolution first reach them?" "Why," I said, "I guess it was when they first heard the drums of the Continentals." *"Drums,"* he said, *"Drums on the Mohawk.* No, you need more movement—*Drums Along the Mohawk."* And there was the title.[8]

The important events depicted in the novel are facts of verifiable history, and Edmonds indicates his debt to various sources that document his story. Among these, he records in his prefatory author's note to his novel and elaborates in a later article in the *Atlantic Monthly,*[9] are such works as Howard Swiggert's *War Out of Niagara: Walter Butler and the Tory Rangers* (1923); W. C. Abbott's *New York in the American Revolution* (1929); William L. Stone's *Life of Joseph Brant—Thayendanegea* (1838); and the *Minute Book of the Committee of Safety* of Tryon County (reprinted 1905). Most of the characters which populate his novel are historical ones; but a few Edmonds invented for purposes of his fiction. These latter include those intrinsically important to his story: Gil and Lana Martin, the young couple who are his primary protagonists; Joe Boleo, a scout; and Sarah McKlennar, an indomitable matriarch whose fiery spirit even the renegade Indians respected. He also invented, he said, the figures of John Weaver, Mary Reall, Mrs. Demooth, Jurry McLonis, Nancy Schuyler, and a few others such as the Indians Gahota and Owigo.

The chronicle history technique worked well in providing a useful framework for the novel. *Drums Along the Mohawk* has a unity, first of all, derived from the chronology which forms its framework—the events of the Revolution in the upstate region; but the author has produced here something considerably more than just another historical novel, for its unity derives from a number of factors, in addition, that are only incidental to the historical context —the pioneering carve-a-home-out-of-the-wilderness life of the newlyweds Gil and Lana Martin; the common bonds existing between the Martins and their fellow settlers and even with such others as Blue Black, one of the missionary Samuel Kirkland's Oneida Indians; the unconsciously derived unity of Mohawk Valley life itself as the settlers face a do-nothing Continental Congress and a military establishment seemingly unconcerned (or ill prepared to be concerned) with local and regional problems even when those problems seriously affect the progress of the war; and a peacock feather, brought to the cabin at Deerfield as Gil and Lana start out life together, taken by Blue Black when their cabin is destroyed by the Seneca Indians in one of the opening rampages in the Mohawk Valley, and returned by Blue Black eight years later when the Martins are again settled at Deerfield. Symbolizing the "reminder of home always in sight" that Mrs. Borst hoped it would provide for her daughter, the peacock feather in its natural simplicity and beauty stands also for the actuality and the potentiality of frontier life.[10]

Walter Edmonds depicts this pioneer life in strongly humanistic terms. In writing about that frontier living, he might, in some ways, be considered a twentieth-century James Fenimore Cooper, but Edmonds's work contains sketches of pioneer life and characterizations that Cooper at his best never achieved. Edmonds's characters, even when met transiently, are *real* people: they surpass frequently in their delineation the Cooper characters who, in the full-stream American romanticism in which the "American Scott" wrote, lacked essential depth. James Russell Lowell's satiric charge in *A Fable for Critics* that Cooper simply drew all his characters from the single mold of his Natty Bumppo was a kind of criticism that could never be levelled at Edmonds, for his characters lead individual lives, and they have individual, all too human traits. Like William Faulkner's, Walter Edmonds's people are flesh-and-blood creations (though admittedly without Faulkner's psychological dimensions or complexity); and they are real people whose problems—however tragic or trivial—are real.

We might add a further note of comparison with William Faulkner, for, like him, Edmonds respects his characters, especially the average citizen caught up in a war he never clearly understands. For both writers their characters are human beings, not artistic stereotypes. The reader may love them or hate them, but he cannot dismiss them as of no consequence. To do so would be to miss the full meaning of Edmonds's writing.

In the circumstances of the times, the smallest detail of life becomes a detail in Edmonds's depiction; and it is one that has consequence. To cite an example: when the McKlennar farm is found to be miraculously untouched following an Indian rampage, Gil, Lana, Mrs. McKlennar, and a few other persons move from the protection of the fort back to the homestead in the open country. It seemed quite safe, for the Indians were reported to be moving westward toward Tioga at the time, and the need for the grain harvest to be accomplished was paramount in the settlers' minds. Everyone worked —the women longer hours than the men, because they also had to attend to the cooking and the washing. In simple storytelling style Edmonds sums up their reaction: "But they all enjoyed it, even the cow, which had been led down from the fort when it was decided to thresh at the farm. The feeling that they were in a house, that they had a place to themselves, made up for all their labor" (p. 520). As a young lass, Mary Weaver, talks about their situation with Mrs. Smith, a wife of one of the sergeants, the author again provides a penetrating insight into the nature not only of frontier life but of basic human involvement during troubled times. The sergeant's wife gently remonstrated Mary's too far-flung ideas:

"You talk about stone houses. Well, all I want to think about is a log house of my own again, and dried punkin and corn ears on the rafters. Just to set down and look at them and know they're mine."

Mary knew how lucky she was without being told. She was growing up. She would be eighteen before long, and John had told her she was getting prettier every day. Her breasts were filling out, and she had more flesh on her shoulders, and her cheeks were rounder. Her legs were still the slim hard legs of a girl; but John liked them, even though he used to tease her about how long they were. "When the war's over," he said one day, "I'm going to buy

you a print dress. I'm going to get it made. With a long skirt. Right
to your toes. Your legs won't show, and you'll be beautiful."
        "I'll powder my hair," she said. "They'll be flour then."
        Imagine it, flour enough to use it on your hair. [Pp. 516–17]

Through such episodes as these, Edmonds tells the story of
the American Revolution through the experiences of the valley settlers. Gilbert Martin serves as the typical settler forced to play the
dual role of breadwinner-farmer and soldier. Rather than focus on the
aristocratic families or the military elite, Edmonds prefers the ordinary farming folk as his central characters; and he provides a log of
what the Revolutionary War was like, and a picture of the Mohawk
Valley during those days. The days are the Mohawk Valley from 1776
to 1784: the American Revolution as it affected the frontier farmers
of the region who unaided withstood the raids of the Iroquois and
the British regulars from Canada.

RECEPTION AND CRITICISM

Hollywood liked it. Not long after *Drums Along the Mohawk* was
published by Little, Brown, film director John Ford's motion picture
was in preparation. Edmonds's vivid portrayal of a colonial couple in
New York's Mohawk Valley proved a lasting Twentieth-Century Fox
production, which still makes the rounds now and then on television's
late show. Lana and Gil were played by Claudette Colbert and Henry
Fonda, who was appearing in his second role based upon an Edmonds's character. Edna May Oliver had the part of Sarah McKlennar in this 1939 production that also saw Ward Bond and John Carradine in principal roles. Both Fonda and Carradine were to join the
cast of yet another Edmonds's novel when *Chad Hanna* was filmed
by Twentieth-Century Fox a short while afterward.
        It seems relevant to note here that during the American Bi-

Advertisement for the motion picture *Drums Along the Mohawk*. Henry
Fonda and Claudette Colbert had the roles of Gil and Lana Martin, a newly-
wed pioneer couple who establish their home in the Mohawk Valley of upstate New York, in this film version of Walter D. Edmonds's novel. Photograph from Movie Star News.

DARRYL F. ZANUCK'S Production of
DRUMS ALONG THE MOHAWK
IN TECHNICOLOR
STARRING
Claudette COLBERT
Henry FONDA
Edna May OLIVER
Eddie COLLINS
John CARRADINE
Dorris BOWDON
Jessie RALPH
Arthur SHIELDS
Robert LOWERY
Roger IMHOF
A 20th CENTURY-FOX PICTURE
DIRECTED BY JOHN FORD
ASSOCIATE PRODUCER Raymond Griffith
SCREEN PLAY BY LAMAR TROTTI AND SONYA LEVIEN — BASED UPON THE NOVEL BY WALTER D. EDMONDS

centennial, motion picture actor Henry Fonda, who had so much to do with the films made from Edmonds's early upstate New York novels, including *Drums Along the Mohawk,* was invited to lead a recreated Tryon County Militia into a re-enactment of the Battle of Oriskany on the 200th anniversary of the August 6, 1777 revolutionary battle. Fonda did not participate, says Montgomery County Historian Anita Smith, but "the re-enactment was exciting. It was seen by 16,000 spectators." The Tryon County Militia is a group of men from the Herkimer County Conservative Alliance, who practiced for the battle re-enactment at the Town of Ohio recreation field, located about thirty miles north of Utica, New York. The militia is named after the eighteenth century Tryon County (subsequently divided into several counties). The march was held beginning at 9 A.M. August 4, 1977, in the village of Herkimer, the site of the revolutionary stronghold, Fort Dayton, one of the prominent settings for portions of Edmonds's novel. The militia followed General Nicholas Herkimer's actual route, ending its three-day march on August 6 at the original Oriskany battlefield. Militias from Canada portrayed the Tory forces of 1777, and numerous other organizations participated in the Oriskany Day 1977 program.

Quite apart from the actor's connection with the motion picture *Drums Along the Mohawk,* there was an even closer bond. Though Henry was born in Nebraska, his ancestors had settled in upper New York State in 1628 and founded the little town which still bears their name. Fonda and the Fondas are, of course, part of Edmonds's Tryon County in the novel.

Some adverse critics of *Drums Along the Mohawk* pointed to Edmonds's frank descriptions of frontier brutality, especially the Indian savagery, and to his failure to compromise by having his characters speak always so as not to offend prudish readers. Edmonds's language is certainly not Howellsian; but, then, Edmonds is not depicting in this novel of revolutionary times a leisure-class society that had time to observe the niceties of convention and the art of refined conversation. The dialogue, like Edmonds's people, is down to earth. A girl who acts in five-letter terms gets called by what her action suggests. And the risqué, earthy dialogue and regional idiom often provide the novel with an element of humor, for *Drums Along the Mohawk* is liberally sprinkled with passages that contain typical Yorker wit—wry, homespun banter that existed in another age.

When Joe Boleo, for example, failed to understand General Nicholas Herkimer's comment that any good officer "has got to keep his line of communications open," the scout rejoined, "My God! What's that?"

> "Well, he don't want anybody cutting in on his trail."
> Joe scratched his head.
> "Oh, you mean he wants to know which way he's going when he has to run home. I thought it was a bowel complaint." [Pp. 146–47]

When Mrs. McKlennar mused about her lost husband, Barney, she always managed to keep a proud face and a stoic, frontier pose. "Mush," she told her companions once. "I remember when Barney went off on Abercrombie's expedition. He kissed me in bed and gave me a wallop behind and said 'You stay here, Sally, old girl, and keep it warm against the time I get back.' He couldn't stand anything sentimental, you see" (pp. 158–59). And when another settler tried to interest Gil Martin in another girl, he couldn't understand Gil's unwillingness to stop his harvesting and join him. "Polly's got a sister that can give you fun," he told Gil.

But the outspoken realism, overt sensationalism, and masochistic descriptions in more contemporary books from John Baldwin to Harold Robbins make the critics of Edmonds's novel seem abnormally squeamish, and Edmonds's diction, by comparison, almost like Louisa May Alcott's. A reviewer in the *Chicago Tribune* called attention to the "Indian savagery incarnate"; but both whites and Indians engaged in atrocities during the Revolution; and part of Edmonds's intention was to show the effect that the long-sustained fear of the Indians had on the settlers of the Mohawk Valley region. Such adverse comments may seem absurd in this day of pornographic excess, but the novel's contemporary critics must be taken in the context of that period.

Edmonds's own defense of his writing offers the novel's best justification, and it was relevant to the novel then, as it is relevant for more recent audiences. "My concern," he wrote, "has been with life as it was; as you or I, our mothers or our wives, our brothers and husbands and uncles, might have experienced it."[11] *Drums Along the Mohawk* is the story of people, *a people,* the settler-farmers of York State; and most of them, quite frankly, would rather have tended their crops than fight a war; yet they found to their frustration that they had to tend their crops *and* fight the war. They are not adventurous Horatio Hornblowers, who find romance in military

Ward Bond, Henry Fonda, and Claudette Colbert as Mohawk Valley settlers during the Revolution, in a scene from *Drums Along the Mohawk,* director John Ford's technicolor film based on the novel by Walter D. Edmonds. Photograph courtesy of Twentieth Century-Fox, copyright © 1939 Twentieth Century-Fox Film Corp. All rights reserved.

things; and they are far removed, both by geography and thinking, from national political figures like Washington, who conduct the war. "Food, crops, games, and weather," says Edmonds, are more important, for these things are closer to them. Yet the valley people do fight a war—and their story is the more dramatic for their doing so under conditions of extreme adversity. For it is these anonymous, ordinary citizens who really create history. In writing the story of their daily record in the days of the American Revolution, Edmonds accomplished what few other historical fictionists achieve so well: a book which not only illustrates and illuminates history which is its basis but which also transcends the limitations of historical fiction to produce quality literature. The author of the historical novel must be, as one critic observed, "a storyteller first: a reflection which suggests why, for so many historical novels, the reading is like plodding knee-deep in snow."[12] Happily, Walter D. Edmonds is a storyteller, first and foremost; and *Drums Along the Mohawk* gives evidence of his unique artistry. The book, in short, is good both as a novel and as history.

Good historical fiction provides a valid corollary to the historian's history, because of its insistence upon unromanticized verity. Popular romance with a historical setting, on the other hand, differs vastly from major historical fiction. Walter Edmonds knows the difference, for as he once wryly put it himself, "the historical romancer is not interested in underwear unless it is a lady's, preferably in the process of removal."[13] The writer of serious historical novels will have none of this. As other literary critics have implied, the historical romance writer generally deals only superficially with history, using the historic event and setting as framing devices only, and the historical personage as a focal point upon which and around which his imagination can have free rein. The author of the valid historical novel, Edmonds noted, "wants to bring into his pages a sense of the present, of the immediacy of events."[14] In such a context even the imaginary characters he might create "belong."

In speaking of his own works Edmonds has said that it "might be better to call them chronicles of the life and times of the ordinary citizens through two hundred-odd years, and the growth and change of their section of Central New York." The famous men of history, he concluded, "are in large part a reflection of their times; but it is the little man behind history who in the long run determines those times."[15] *Drums Along the Mohawk* assuredly ranks high among the works which best present this sense of history.

6

Upstate, Downstate

HE SUCCESS OF *DRUMS ALONG THE MOHAWK* assured Walter D. Edmonds a firm position among the writers of American historical fiction, and it gave him further popular appeal through the movies. His interest continued to focus upon New York State history, culture, and people; but for his next novel he put aside the Revolutionary War era and the stirring themes suggested by the epical Erie Canal accomplishment, which he had treated in earlier novels and short stories. He was later to return to both of these subjects briefly in the late 1940s, when he wrote a couple of short novels about frontier life, *In the Hands of the Senecas* (1947) and *Wilderness Clearing* (1949), and a final Erie novel—actually a novelette—*The Wedding Journey* (1947). He had a different setting for *Young Ames* (1942), in which he dealt with the days of mercantile life downstate in bustling New York City. Following this, Edmonds turned once again, as he did in *The Big Barn*, his second novel, to the particular region of his birth, the upstate New York country around Boonville. With *The Boyds of Black River* (1953), one of his most endearing novels, he wrote about an upstate family at the turn of the century. But in 1940 there was some "Erie" in *Chad Hanna*, when Edmonds turned his talents to revivifying the days of the roving circus troupes in the middle of the nineteenth century in central New York.

THE CIRCUS IN UPSTATE NEW YORK: *CHAD HANNA*

Edmonds explained in an acknowledgment to *Chad Hanna* that "the first purpose . . . is the entertainment of the reader," and certainly that purpose is delightfully fulfilled: no serious problems of a portentous social nature are to be found in the novel. "Ladies and Gentlemen," wrote one reviewer caught up in the carnival spirit which the book evokes, "here is 'Chad Hanna,' unparalleled novel about the circus by the unsurpassed master of fiction about the Erie Canal, Walter D. Edmonds. You'll read it and weep; you'll read it and laugh; you'll read it and chuckle."[1] The exuberance of the reviewer is not without sound basis, for Edmonds in *Chad Hanna* (1940) presented a novel rich in Americana. The reader cannot easily dismiss the novel or its hero. Chad is young America; he is vibrant and vital, both as a character and symbol; and he emerges in our minds with a sense of that inimitable past when traveling circuses like the Huguenine's roamed New York State and theatrical troupes trod the boards, as they said, from town to frontier town, "bringing illusion and delight," as another Yorker novelist put it, "to the dark fringes of civilization."[2]

Prior to book publication in 1940, *Chad Hanna* appeared as "Red Wheels Rolling" in serial installments in the *Saturday Evening Post*. The story went quickly to Hollywood, thus following *Rome Haul* ("The Farmer Takes a Wife") and *Drums Along the Mohawk*. Twentieth-Century Fox brought it to the screen. Nunnally Johnson wrote the screenplay for the film version, which saw Henry Fonda in his third Edmonds's role. He was cast, of course, as Chad, the young hero. Linda Darnell had the role of Caroline, a girl who early in the novel befriends Chad; and Dorothy Lamour, as a bareback rider Albany Yates, formed the romantic triangle necessary to the times. Guy Kibbee, Jane Darwell, and John Carradine—all veteran actors—rounded out the well-chosen cast.

What artistry *Chad Hanna* possesses as a work of fiction lies in the author's realistic regionalism, in his full recreation of the circus atmosphere of a bygone era, and, above all, in his catching the underlying human comedy of circus life in the early nineteenth century. The death of Oscar the lion, the fight between the two rival circuses, Huguenine's and Burke's, the very character of Canastota's Elias Proops, and the human warmth of Mrs. Huguenine—to cite a few of the myriad elements comprising the novel—provide rich evi-

Announcement of the television re-release of the motion picture *Chad Hanna*, adapted from Walter D. Edmonds's 1940 novel of a touring circus troupe in the nineteenth century. Press sheet from National Telefilm Associates, Inc.

dence of the author's sense of pathos and humor which pervades the pages of this book.

Edmonds's characters exist comfortably in a world suited to them. They fall neither in the stereotype mold of James Fenimore Cooper's pioneer life romanticism nor in the intellectualized zones more patrician authors demanded of their creations. Edmonds's characters are real, though they may lack depth at times. "It is interesting to think how this author has captured a locale and a period of time," commented a reviewer in *Library Journal*, and a writer in the *Yale Review* allowed that this "is the way Americans must have talked in those days."[3] It is not difficult to assume that circus folk had an easy-going, light-hearted philosophy—they were that breed of men and women—whose very existence and livelihood depended upon people liking them. To depict this kind of person, the fictionist must sacrifice characters with strength and depth in delineation for the more important (that is, the more "realistic") purpose of presenting them as parts of a milieu. Edmonds's dedication to historical accuracy and his indefatigable research are again evident; and he drew his characters in the only way they could be validly depicted. The 1830s was the age of the common man, not of individual men. In writing *Chad Hanna* Edmonds made no compromise; his characters belong.

Edmonds's offer of *Chad Hanna* as "entertainment," in his preface, is overly modest, for the novel is more than that. The book provides, in regional tones, a good delineation of the age-old question of maturity, a frequent theme with Edmonds, particularized in this instance to that of a carefree youth of the 1830s rising to the responsibilities of manhood. Just as Jerry Fowler in *Erie Water* matured as the Grand Erie Canal reached completion, so in *Chad Hanna* the young Chad finds his place and his maturity when the circus with which he casts his lot rises above its troubles and finds stability. The roisterous days of a growing New York State come to vivid life with Edmonds's typewriter. The characterizations are firm, sure, as in *Rome Haul;* and while Edmonds's narrative style on occasion suffers from the conglomerate effect of an overpopulated landscape that some critics feel mars the structure of his novels, the story line here is clearer and more continuous, the action more unified; Edmonds's control of the story falters less than in earlier works, and the historic verisimilitude functions as it should to provide a regional backdrop which serves to reinforce rather than to overwhelm the plot. *Chad Hanna* is good regional fiction.

Opening in the mid-1830s, the narrative of the novel shifts

its locale with the moves of "Huguenine's Great and Only International Circus" as it rolls from village to village, hamlet to hamlet, throughout central upstate New York. The sprawling Erie Canal, stretching from Albany to Buffalo, is there as a backdrop, a kind of benevolent "old friend" that represents a stability and the only real home the orphaned Chad knew. But *Chad Hanna* is not a canal novel. What Edmonds does is depict the circus, just as Samuel Hopkins Adams was later to do for the roving theatrical troupes in his novel, *Banner by the Wayside* (1947). The show's the thing, and with the gusto and style of a Sam Clemens, Edmonds revivifies the age of shows:

> ... By ten o'clock on Monday morning, Elias Proops admitted that Canastota looked like a real metropolis. Wagons were hitched all along the street. They said the church sheds were jam full of horses. . . .
>
> The day was perfect: circus weather, Mr. Bisbee said. . . . Everywhere through the village out-of-town folks were visiting on the front porches. Their voices up and down Peterboro Street made a sound as steady as flowing water. Once in a while the pitch changed, and then you could see a circus performer threading his way along the footpath.
>
> Down beyond Hitchcock's Professor Arganave had set up a Hydro-Oxygen Gas Microscope. He had five slides, which cost ten cents to look at. One was a sample of blood from a young unmarried girl, the second was from a married woman; the third was the blood from a healthy man; after it you saw the blood from a man who had died of drink. (The professor said he had got it from Bellevue Hospital in New York. Judd Parsons, ordering a double whiskey in the Yellow Bud, declared it was enough to shake a man's nerves.) The most interesting to see was the fifth—the blood of a man-eating lion. The professor explained that it had been taken from the lion in Huguenine's Circus. If you looked close you could see islands of human blood in the slide, proving the fact beyond a doubt. For twenty-five cents you could see the blood of half a dozen celebrated people, like Byron, or Benjamin Franklin, or Alexander Hamilton (procured at Weehawken just after he was shot by Aaron Burr). For fifty cents the professor would take a sample of your blood and let you compare the slide with those of the others. Canastota had never seen anything like it. [Pp. 110–111][4]

Chad soon gives up the canal town, Canastota, for the more appealing circus. Boyishly indolent and independent, Chad befriends Henry Prince, a runaway slave. Unlike Mark Twain's work (Edmonds has been unjustly criticized for his), the novel fails to develop Chad's position with regard to the Negro beyond his finding himself on the side of abolition and, pragmatically, making some small change of the "nigger-chasers" in the doing. The Henry Prince episode serves as no more than an opening interlude, enabling the hero to meet up with the circus and with Caroline Trid, the daughter of a rapscallious canaller whose means of livelihood are far from respectable.[5] Caroline Trid and Chad Hanna follow the circus, and they eventually marry, though their lives and the fortunes of the circus are complicated by an equestrienne of fine figure and considerable opportunistic bent who provides the story's love triangle.

The circus owner's wife, Mrs. Huguenine, plays a strong part throughout the story, as mother-confessor to Caroline, Chad, and the whole troupe. She has affinities with other Edmonds's women, notably Big-Foot Sal of the earlier short story, and with Ma Halleck and Mrs. Gurget of previous novels. All are cut from the same cloth.[6]

Once on his own, Chad's native intelligence and natural managerial capabilities procure him his advancement in the circus. "Chad knows a lot too," acknowledged Mr. Huguenine, the circus owner. "He's pretty near as good as I am. . . . He acts responsible" (p. 380). Chad does, in general, act responsible, a trait which becomes a hallmark in the Edmonds's canon. Like Mark Twain's Huckleberry Finn, Chad is basically and naively moral. Like Huck, he is practical, pragmatic, and resourceful, albeit unsophisticated. It is Chad who gets the idea to disguise Huguenine's wagon with haycocks to fool the pursuing competitor circus trying to run Huguenine's out of business. It is Chad who rides with the competitor's parade and leads the townspeople astray—right to the Huguenine's lot instead! It is Chad who, at the beginning of the novel, plans the escape of the Negro runaway and insures its success. And it is Chad who conceives the preposterous idea to turn catastrophe into advantage by exhibiting the deceased Oscar as "the only dead lion in captivity in the United States" (p. 385).

Folkloristic touches like the latter abound in *Chad Hanna*. In their essential credibility, the tall tales Edmonds works into his narrative are worthy of Twain: the circusman who caught his ankle in a peg of the big tent during a windstorm that lifted him a hundred feet in the air and brought him down "sprang in the middle of the Mississippi River," with the big top itself "full enough of catfish to

In full circus garb Guy Kibbee in his role as the owner of Huguenine's Circus in the Twentieth Century-Fox production of *Chad Hanna*. The film also featured Jane Darwell as Mrs. Huguenine and John Carradine as Bisbee, along with stars Henry Fonda, Dorothy Lamour, and Linda Darnell. Photograph courtesy of Twentieth Century-Fox, copyright © 1940 Twentieth Century-Fox Film Corp. All rights reserved.

feed the entire company" (pp. 160–61); the great hoax of exhibiting the dead lion, later to bury him in Avon because the odor became "so powerful that half a bottle of Mrs. Huguenine's perfumery barely dented it" (p. 389); and the finding of the strong man who was fired from his job with the Erie Railroad "because he wanted to drive spikes and he hit so hard he made dents in the iron rails" (p. 437). In such instances Walter Edmonds continues in the twentieth century the tradition of the frontier humorists of the nineteenth.

It all happens in Jacksonian America, an era which much appeals to Edmonds. In that time period, as fellow novelist and historian Hervey Allen put it, progress swooped drunkenly forward. Politics rarely get a line in *Chad Hanna*, but one feels the sympathies of the author nonetheless. The very ambitions of the struggling circus reflect the spirit of the nation in the growing pains days of the early nineteenth century. At that time New York was still the frontier, for it was to many people, especially those in New England, "the West." The circus becomes a cultural force in pushing back the frontier: "Why, there's places out that way where they've never even *heard* of elephants!" (p. 546). At the novel's close Chad's vision symbolically unites the expansionist America as the circus with its menagerie walks the streets "from Herkimer to the Mississippi River" (p. 548).

YOUNG AMES: THE BUSINESS WORLD IN JACKSONIAN AMERICA

In his sixth novel, *Young Ames* (1942), Edmonds left the upstate New York setting of his previous works for the mercantile scene of New York City. John Ames's story parallels in time, however, Chad Hanna's adventures with the roving circus troupe. The literary departure of the author from the Mohawk Valley area did not mark the creation of either a character or a story as well delineated as in the former novel. While there is a good deal of entertainment value to *Young Ames*, the plot is awfully contrived, and the situations so filled with incredible coincidences that even for a story set in Jacksonian America with its anything-is-possible atmosphere, the story of the rise of the young hero to prominence in New York's commercial world becomes almost a satire on itself. Even so, one must admit that Edmonds's storyteller technique works its charm, for *Young Ames* is fun to read.

In the first sixteen pages young John Ames, who is so constantly referred to as "young Ames" that the reader can become tired of the reiteration, gets a job as a junior clerk in a well-known commercial house, saves the firm four or five hundred dollars on a transaction, decides he will be a junior partner in three years' time, and sees the girl he knows he is going to marry though he doesn't know her name. When the girl turns out to be the daughter of the firm's senior partner, the stage is set for the typical Horatio Alger rags-to-riches tale.

In *Young Ames*, perhaps, Edmonds is a bit out of his element away from the upstate countryside and its history. The only connection in this novel with more typical Edmonds materials seems to be in John Ames's coming originally from Troy, New York, where the Mohawk River joins the Hudson, and in the period of the novel a terminus of the Erie Canal. John Ames himself differs from earlier Edmonds heroes in his lacking the warmly human touches that mark so many of his characters as real people. By contrast to Chad Hanna, Dan Harrow, and Gil Martin, John Ames is less artfully developed and more artificially the stereotype. The original stories about young Ames, which appeared in various issues of the *Saturday Evening Post,* would probably have sufficed, as some critics of the book noted. In their several parts the stories made sense as light contributions to the magazine literature of the thirties; as a novel they do not necessarily add up all that well. Nonetheless it is entertaining, and Edmonds' trip down to Gotham is a light-hearted literary journey.

A dialogue between young Ames and Gibbs, his best friend at Chevelier, Deming & Post, his employers, indicates the nature of both character and plot. "You know just about everything, don't you Johnny?" said Gibbs.

> . . . "You have to keep your ears open if you're going to make money in New York," young Ames said complacently. "I've got to make a lot."
> . . . "Do you ever think about anything else, Johnny?"
> . . . "I don't like being poor. I want to get on top. It's going to take longer than I thought, maybe, but I'll get there." [P. 166]

If, however, one considers *Young Ames* another entry in Edmonds's stories about young America and individual enterprise, then he can at least enjoy the story. Despite the naivete, there's something stirring in the meeting between young John Ames, while on a trip to Washington, D.C., for the firm, and Andrew Jackson, president of the United States, as the young man takes a walk in one of the city's jewelry shops, a voice nearby says "Good evening, Sir."

> "Good evening." Young Ames looked up with a start. He had heard no one coming; he had expected no one to come long this walk so far below the White House. It was nearly dark, and the bench was in an almost hidden corner. Then as he looked at the tall figure leaning on the cane, he scrambled to his feet.
> The man raised his hand. "Sit down, sir. I didn't intend to disturb you. I saw you were looking at a pin."
> "Yes, sir." Young Ames stammered a little. "It's just a pin I bought for a friend."
> He stared at the thin pale face, with its straight features and clear eyes and white hair showing below the hat brim.
> "Would you let me see it?"
> He took the box from young Ames's hand and held it close to his eyes.
> "It's pretty," he said. "Whoever she is, she'll surely like it."
> "Do you think so, sir? It's not much of a pin."
> "She's worth a good deal more," young Ames said quickly.
> "Then she's sure to like it. Sit down sir. Do you mind if I sit down also? I've done my walk and there's still a few minutes till dinner. My name's Andrew Jackson."
> "Mine's John Ames." [Pp. 268–69]

In this casual, matter-of-fact way, John Ames meets the president of the United States. Perhaps this is the way it was—or could have been—in an earlier America. Possibly Edmonds is suggesting through the actions of President Jackson that this is the way it always should be in America, even when it is not. The chance meeting becomes, in a sense, the making of young Ames, for Jackson's down-to-earth simplicity makes a strong impression on the youth, who heretofore half believed—and followed when he did not stop to think—the anti-Jackson myths which New York's financial world circulated about the man in the White House. Jackson's essential Americanism appeals especially to the romantic and optimistic Ames. Using as his symbolic American a Mississippi riverboatman whom young Ames had met at one time, the president expresses his plea for the democratic ideal:

"There's your fire-eater. He's your real American. He can yell louder, fight harder, and laugh louder than fifty sinners, but he's as good a gentlemen as John Forsyth. But you couldn't persuade some of a small class we have here in this country that he wasn't half-alligator. Those people haven't outgrown Europe yet, Mr. Ames. They got what they wanted out of the Revolution, but now they want to sit down. This country can't ever sit down. I've been in parlors in Boston and New York it was an honor to go into, but I tell you the knicknacks on the mantel piece had a better idea of the American Eagle than the human occupants. He's a bird you can't keep perched. He only looks like something when he's on the wing." [P. 271]

When the conversation gets around to the impending conflict with France and the financiers' fears that Jackson will deliver a speech which will anger King Louis Philippe to war, the president gives young Ames the moral he has been searching for throughout the book.

... "The money's not worth fighting for. Money never is. But we're a young country, and Europe, like some of our seaboard classes, still thinks of us as a small line of disunited states. They'll have to be shown we have a sense of our own dues. No, Mr. Ames, you don't have to kill a man because he owes you the price of a horse."

For Jackson, it's the pragmatic realization that, in a democracy especially, the collective public opinion of a united people counts. "Public opinion is the one thing, no matter what they say," said Jackson, "that even emperors are afraid of. If it's united. We've got to show ours is united. ... So they'll be no war, but ... ," the general added dryly, "there won't be any doubt about our views. The American people must learn that if they stand together, they can lick the world" (p. 272).

One other figure in the novel provides the final catalytic element in the maturing of Ames. The firm's chief clerk, McVitty, a fifty-year employee who bores people with his proverbs and moral quotations, finally proves to be among the young man's most loyal supporters. Old McVitty trained young Ames without sentiment, but he trained him well for succeeding in the business world. It is McVitty who, after Ames's engagement to Christine Chevelier is a *fait accompli* and the young man's continued business acumen had paid off by his bringing in "the Downey account" which even the partners had never been able to secure, calls Ames aside and fills him in on the real meaning of *reputation*. He shows young Ames the ledgers of the company from the initial transactions made in 1782 by old Ferdinand Chevelier, the firm's founder, down from the time McVitty's own hand took over the books on August 19, 1784.

The lesson young Ames sees in the ledgers and learns from McVitty is one of loyalty and reputation. That lesson, which (Edmonds seems to be saying) everyone must learn, is the essential one of growing up with a sense of knowing right from wrong and of knowing, too, how to make the decisions that will create a purposeful meaningful life, not only for the individual but for those with whom he comes into contact. There's something of *The Rise of Silas Lapham*, finally, about Edmonds's *Young Ames,* for Lapham's moral rise, while much more universally applicable and much more substantially drawn by William Dean Howells, is nonetheless reflected in Ames's decision to turn down the offer of Mr. Downey which would have doubled his salary on the spot and given him the interest and commissions he could easily have used. In the climactic events of John Ames's story, a fire that destroys most of the commercial district of lower Manhattan is especially disastrous for the firm of Chevelier, Deming & Post; the two junior partners leave the firm, Post taking his money with him to join a competitor company and leaving Chevelier almost completely bankrupt; and at this very point it is young Ames—now young only in years—who sticks with the owner and begins earnestly to build a new commercial house on the foundation of the old. In this, then, Edmonds has captured something of the American story, and Chevelier & Co. emerges as the final symbol of a characteristically American success tale.

AT BOYD HOUSE: AN EDMONDS MASTERPIECE

"Ours is in no way an impressive landscape," wrote Edmonds in *The Boyds of Black River,* "but there are more woods than farmland in it, and besides the river, it is full of springs and running brooks; and, perhaps, if you are born in it, as I had been, it gains meaning" (p. 154). The meaning of the upstate North Country of Edmonds's own experience comes through nowhere more surely than in the pages of this novel published in 1953. *The Boyds of Black River* is not so much a novel, actually, as a series of loosely knit narratives about the Boyd family, as seen from the viewpoint to Teddy Armond, the Boyds' Boonville neighbor.

In contrast to other novels, Edmonds in this work chose to deal with relatively few characters, and he allowed them to develop thoroughly. Uncle Ledyard Boyd, the patriarch of the family, and his gouty old friend, Admiral Porter, serve to present the critical comments, sometimes contemptuous and sometimes stabilizing, of the "older generation." As an authentically drawn upstater, Uncle Ledyard has no counterpart in literature, save for the deliberately more talkative Grandfather in Samuel Hopkins Adams's *Grandfather Stories*, which, as with all of Adams's later work, indirectly shows the influence of Edmonds. The housekeeper at Boyd House, a woman who kept things in commotion with the spirit of her Irish forebears, succeeds "only in raising the dust and making an unholy turbulence. The trouble was that she was a born cook, and Uncle Ledyard took her food as the stuff of heaven it was and accepted her airs and her racket along with it . . ." (p. 10). Her husband, John Callant, serves as chief farmhand for the Boyds; and both the Callants, man and wife, form a natural part of the household. Young Doone Boyd, who like Uncle Ledyard lives only for horses, and Kathy O'Chelrie, who married him, round out the central figures, all of whom are seen by young Armond in his close relationship with Boyd House. Teddy is both an observer and a participant; one suspects, very reasonably, he is Edmonds himself.

The principal role in this story of Boyd House really belongs to Kathy, the Admiral's pretty daughter, whose elopement with Doone Boyd forms the climactic event of the opening narrative. She becomes, as an essential outsider, the foil to Doone; and through her presence the events of the novel are unified. From the time she and Doone fall in love to the final narrative in which the temporary threat of Candida Brown's blonde artificiality is faced, her warmth and charm pervade the scenes or serve as quiet background to them.

Edmonds continued in this novel to be the storyteller and yarnspinner, always with a firm regard for native lore and regional idiom. Woven into the fabric of *The Boyds of Black River* are numerous incidental episodes and situations which provoke a chuckle or provide a warmly human insight into character: the bet between Uncle Ledyard and the Admiral over whether or not Doone will fall in love with Kathy; the race between Doone's Blue Dandy and the Admiral's automobile, which ends in the young couple's elopement; the fantastic humor of a farrowing sow holding up the Admiral's drive while she gave birth to twenty-seven piglets in the middle of the road; the catching of Old Ephraim, the legendary deer; the Admiral's hiring a runner to go back and forth between the race track and his daughter's hospital bedside, ready to bring her news of his winning a race and him news of a grandchild.

The six episodes or chapters deal with various incidents in the lives of the Boyds, an unsophisticated North Country family whose inheritance—of farm, of name, and of a sense of tradition— pervades the narrative. In one, it is the story of Kathy's return from a theater-centered life in New York and Long Island to the Black River of her childhood, to fan the flame of love she knows is in Doone Boyd, spite his rural, taciturn manner and an intense preoccupation with horses and farm life. Another episode involves a race track tale that is suspenseful and well conceived. One chapter deals with Candida Brown's intrusion into the domestic and natural tranquility of Boyd House; and one episode is primarily Teddy's.

The importance of Teddy Armond's place is integral, of course, to the overall structure of the *The Boyds of Black River*, for he is the narrator-observer. The chapter dealing with Teddy and his dog, a pedigreed four-year-old bull terrier named Leonidas, lets the reader view this narrator-observer in a situation of critical importance in his own life. Originally published in the *Saturday Evening Post* as "Honor of the County," Edmonds's account of Teddy's involving his pet Leonidas won praise from the critics. Although ostensibly a story about a dog fight, one reviewer reported:

> It really covers a great deal of ground in several directions: the love of a boy for his dog; the subtle appeal made to him to accept "manly" standards; the breakdown of the boy when he sees the dog really about to fight and the effect of impressing upon him that having made the bargain he must go through with it; the boy's feeling of guilt toward the dog, and the dog's large "humanity" in forgiving the unnecessary punishment inflicted upon him.[7]

The scene at Bender's barn to which Teddy reluctantly brings Leonidas for the match with a drummer's dog, Slasher, shows Edmonds's typical regard for detail and descriptive realism:

... There must have been thirty or forty men clustered round an open space in the middle of the wagon run. The smoke from their pipes mounted lethargically past my face and drifted out into the shadows of the empty mows. The lanterns they carried showed me every detail of their faces, but even the faces I recognized I did not seem to know. Some were eager, some tense with the money involved, some insane from the whiskey their wearers had passed down, some were openly savage and one or two were cool and taking stock. But all wore a strange mask-like quality, as if it had been painted on by the lantern light. And their voices were lustful, and as I listened to the bandied estimations of the dogs, and to the bets going one way and another, it seemed to me that I was losing my hold on the world, and that the valley I lived in wasn't the Black River Valley I had always thought it was, but an alien place, and I a stranger in it. [P. 89]

"It's the honor of the county is in it," John Callant told him, and Teddy Armond learns morality and responsibility in his acquiescence, the acceptance of the bargain made.

The novel thus revolves around Teddy. As with other Edmonds characters here and there throughout his works, the young boy sees the world with Huckleberry Finn eyes, the sensitivity of youth coupled with the common sense of one who without consciously being aware of it knows himself to be a part of a tradition that has always been individualistic and self-sufficient. The *Boyds of Black River* bears at least a resemblance, in this sense, to major works in the American literary tradition, like *Huckleberry Finn* and *The Catcher in the Rye,* that utilize a youth as the narrator-hero; and Edmonds's importance in doing for New York regionalism what Mark Twain and J. D. Salinger have done for other areas of literature should not be overlooked. But, more importantly, *The Boyds of Black River* has a literary kinship to William Faulkner's novels of Yoknapatawpha, for Edmonds' depiction of a tradition, rooted in native soil, and of characters maintaining it in upstate New York easily brings to mind Faulkner's saga of southern landowners, the activities of the Comsons, the DeSpains and their associates in *The Unvanquished* and *The Big Woods.*

Like *The Unvanquished* and *The Big Woods,* the episodes in Edmonds's novel are only loosely related, but their totality presents an aggregate meaning of a place, a time, and—perhaps it can be said without too much exaggeration—a people, or at least a way of life that is characteristically north country in the early 1900s. Edmonds shares with Faulkner a sense of the soil, along with a concomitant sensitivity to nature. Characters like Uncle Ledyard and Doone Boyd smell of "horses and tobacco and clean hay" (p. 5). They are hunters, like Faulkner's McCaslins in "The Bear," annually going after the great buck who has become a legend, "Old Ephraim," with horns like a brush pile. They are fishermen, who know the perfect time for bass with "the moon not yet up the water grey with a very slight ripple" (p. 55), arguing the merits of a red and white fly over a royal coachman. Like Faulkner, Edmonds captures in broadly humanistic terms the sensibilities of his people, for also, as with Faulkner, the characters *are* his people. He has that sense of the past which sees history as formed of people and civilization fashioned by their birthrights in the land, with a continuity extending from the days of the Indians to the present.

> . . . Title to the land was to Julian Boyd from the State of New York, and that Bounty Right together with a bill of sale signed by Mr. Boyd and five Indians in council marking the transfer of two thousand acres as for a rifle, a set of razors, a quilted dressing gown, and one barrel of whiskey, was all title they needed to show so long as they kept up the back pages of the family Bible that ended with Doone's name. [P. 14]

Refreshingly, one finds that there is in the Edmonds's novel a lightness and a warmth lacking in much of the Faulkner canon. There is none of the Compson or Sartoris degeneration even remotely possible at Boyd House, because the past is not an embittering survival in upstate New York. "It was long ago," says Edmonds with profound simplicity at the end of the book, "and it seems unreal in this world of today. . . . We were all in love, whatever our age" (p. 284).

7

Shorter Novels and Children's Books

*B*ECAUSE HE IS PRIMARILY AN ARTIST," wrote Dayton Kohler in the *English Journal,* "the work of Walter D. Edmonds goes beyond a local realism. Beneath his faithful use of local color he attempts to express the essential truths of human experience."[1] This is perhaps one reason why Edmonds's stories so often appeal to young readers, even when he is writing for adults. It is true especially in his novelettes and other shorter pieces either written for young readers or adapted in format for them. In addition to the major fiction already surveyed, Edmonds published numerous shorter books that have evoked the same response from the reviewers and critics as have his major novels. Of his shorter novels, two—*The Wedding Journey* and *In the Hands of the Senecas*—were Atlantic Monthly Press books. Of his "minor" books of fiction, some are slight and some are serious, some recall themes of his major novels, and some—the earlier children's books—are actually adult short stories republished as books for young readers.

THE WEDDING JOURNEY

For *The Wedding Journey* (1947) Edmonds returned to one of his favorite subjects, the Erie Canal, as he placed two young newlyweds aboard the canal packetboat *Western Lion* at Schenectady, New York, bound for Buffalo and Ohio. The title suggests comparison be-

105

tween this work and that of William Dean Howells's novel, *Their Wedding Journey* (1872), although in Howells's book his bride and groom, Isabel and Basil March, ride the trains rather than the slow-moving canal boats, as they travel across New York State to Niagara Falls and Canada. Actually, albeit superficially, Edmonds's *The Wedding Journey* does bring another Howells book to mind: Howells's more famous *The Rise of Silas Lapham.* In Edmonds's story, as in the Howells novel, it is the seemingly less-favored sister who leads the young man to the altar.[2]

Once aboard the canal packetboat, the bride meditates as she looks at her reflection in the mirror of the ladies' washroom.

> But it did not satisfy her at all. She wished it could have been blond and beautiful like her sister's. Clorinda was the kind of girl that people looked at. As Aunt Francine had often said, "There's nothing statuesque about Bella." All the family had expected, when Roger first came to call, that he had his eye on Clorinda. Even Clorinda hadn't troubled to deny it. The fact that it was now Bella who found herself . . . the wife of Roger Willcox, seemed utterly, delightfully incredible. [P. 5]

The novelette is rather Howellsian, one must conclude after all, for it rolls along as placidly as the barely ruffled waters. Edmonds's depiction is unhurried, almost like that of a painting of the packet, its passengers, and of the canal on which Captain Harrow's boat takes the travelers. "Everything is there, but all is remote," said the *New York Times.* "Richard LeGallienne would have liked it. Stevenson, too."[3]

The story is charming—if that word can be used in a not disparaging way—and the scenes of life in a slower-paced age are withal accurate. Nostalgia hangs over the book, of course, for one feels inevitably the twinge of the romantic's remorse at the passing of the times when, to use the canal idiom, the world went at four miles an hour. One must have an essential rapport with the times and should remember his history to find this Edmonds's novel rewarding. To say simply that it is quaint is to oversimplify Edmonds. *The Wedding Journey* is *sincerely* quaint, and that makes the difference. When Roger Willcox, with the impatience of youth and his new status as a married man, urges the captain to make the trip from Schenectady to Buffalo in four days, Captain Harrow tells him, "Four days? Well, I'll give you a run for your money, mister. Maybe I'll shade it under four days. It's a light trip and we're out to bust time wide open. The company's given me a hundred dollars to pay my fines for speeding" (p. 19). Far removed from this jet age, *The Wedding Journey* makes a reader wonder if there ever really was a time when a canal packet could be fined for exceeding the four-mile-an-hour limit imposed by the canal commissioners.

There's story, too, in the novel, but it doesn't flutter pulses and it may not amount to much. It has no covert symbolism, this novel. No sociological drama. No Freudian implications. Mrs. Willcox put it rightly, as she caught sight of the famed bridge across the Mohawk River as the canal boat left Schenectady. Leaving behind that great landmark of early America, Bella "felt the world unfolding for her as the water unfolded for the packet's bow" (p. 21). For the reader of *The Wedding Journey* the world of 1835—or at least that part of it along New York State's Grand Western Canal—unfolds, too. It's a refreshing human experience.

MORE *DRUMS ALONG THE MOHAWK*

Contrasting sharply with the pervasive placidity of *The Wedding Journey*, Edmonds's *In the Hands of the Senecas*, also published in 1947, and *Wilderness Clearing*, which came out in 1949, deal with the Indian and white conflicts on the frontier in upstate New York. The first book consists of a series of loosely related narratives that present the varying reactions of pioneer women to being held captive by the savages.

In the Hands of the Senecas, like several other of Edmonds's books, is a novel made up of episodes and stories originally published separately in the *Saturday Evening Post*. The general theme binding these episodes together is the Indians' attack on Dygartsbush, a small community of fifteen families located near Fort Herkimer, and the capture of several of the settlers by the Seneca Indians. The captives included one man, Honus Kelly, two young children, Pete Kelly and Ellen Mitchell, and several women of Dygartsbush—old Mrs. Staats, who is killed assisting Honus to escape; Delia, wife of John Borst, less than a month married when she is taken captive; Caty Breen, hired help at the Kelly house in the village, whom the other women always considered "trash"; and Martha Dygart, who was to endure her bondage under Gekeashsawsa, the Wildcat, head woman of the Indian lodge at Chenandoanes to which she was taken. *In the Hands of the Senecas* is thus essentially the story of the captives and of their endurance; but Edmonds displays throughout an objectivity, as both storyteller and historian, which makes the book a valid chronicle of a harsh kind of Indian-white relationship on the warring frontier in Revolutionary New York.

Following an initial chapter, "The Captives," dealing with the Indian assault on Dygartsbush, he allows in turn each of the figures of Caty Breen, Delia Borst, Martha Dygart, and Ellen Mitchell to serve as a focal center; their varied reactions to the situation of bondage give the reader a penetrating insight into the times in a way which goes beneath the surface of historic generalization. In such delineation the human side of history can be experienced in Edmonds's tale. Delia Borst serves as the unifying character, for her story of a young bride (John Borst, her husband, survived the Dygartsbush massacre by absence from the village on the day of the attack) wed to the Indian Gasotena closes only at the final chapter when she is reunited with her husband John, who ultimately must know her as one who lived as an Indian's squaw and bore her Indian captor a son.

The chapter devoted to Ellen Mitchell is a sympathetic portrayal, as two children, Peter, fourteen, and Ellen, a few months younger, are adopted by Skanasunk and his aged wife Newataquaah, in their remote village of Tecarnohs on the Allegheny. The woman Newataquaah explained it all to Ellen one day:

> "Tecarnohs is a little village and far off from the big trails. But it is good hunting country and we have enough to eat and we do not see many white traders so there are not many drunken people. We are able to keep the old ways. My first husband was an old man. I married him when I was fourteen years old. He died after a while; he was a wise man. Then Skanasunk's mother wished him to marry me. He is a young man. From my first husband I learned how to be wise. When I die Skanasunk will have had time to find his wisdom. Then if he likes he will marry a young girl. So we are not unhappy." She gave Ellen her sidelong smile. "But now we have children. We are both very happy now." [P. 140]

Both Peter and Ellen felt "happy" too; and even when the time came the advancing Continental Army passed within a mile of Tecarnohs and almost all the Indians had left for Niagara, they de-

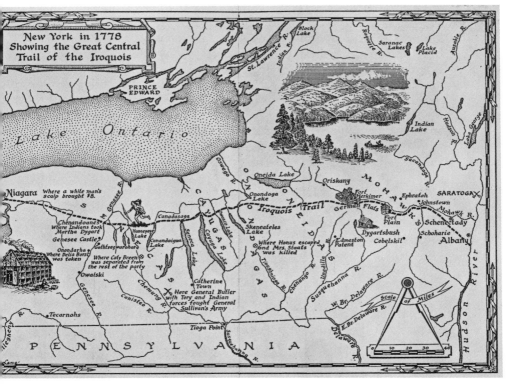

From *In the Hands of the Senecas* by Walter D. Edmonds. Copyright 1947 by
Walter D. Edmonds. Reprinted by permission of Little, Brown and Company.

cided to stay with Skanasunk, though they feared that all the Indians would not remain kindly toward them. As the war intensified,
and disease felled most of the remaining villagers, including Newataquaah, they did finally run off, fearful of Skanasunk's new interest in
the maturing Ellen. As the children came upon the hills south of the
German Flats, they found a feathered arrow stuck in the ground,
with Newataquaah's brooch nearby. Their foster father had followed
them and then left them with a parting gift as they neared Fort
Herkimer.

Nowhere does the author let the interest of the reader lag.
The pace of the action is felt, whether it is the assault of the Indians,
the fear the captives have, the torturous bondage they endure, or the

many minor incidents which let him know that people are Edmonds's subject, whether white or Indian. The two children find they "belong" in Tecarnohs, and they decide to stick it out. Delia Borst bears her Indian captor a son and finds the words of her Indian mate's grandmother if not comforting at least understandable and meaningful. Caty Breen, hired help among the whites, becomes a woman in the eyes of those whom earlier she found only condescension. Old Mrs. Staats proves that beneath a veneer of aristocracy she is nonetheless a woman of the frontier. The Indians are eloquent, as when Gasotena speaks of the founding of the Long House, the League of the Six Nations, and calls the roll of the founders; they are mean, like the wildcat who mercilessly bedevils Martha Dygart, or the marauders at Dygartsbush in the opening chapter; they are warmly wise, like the woman whom Delia Borst came to call "Ucsote," Grandmother, or Newataquaah, who looks after Peter and Ellen as though they were her own children. Finally, they are pathetic, as Delia Borst finds when she looks at the tribal group at Onondarha, after Gasotena's impassioned recounting of the heritage of the Six Nations and the coming of the war between the British and the colonials. She saw it in "their painted faces and outlandish clothes" as they prepared a war party. But perhaps the larger pathos lay in the circumstances themselves, of a people fighting for land once so open to them, used by one alien people as convenient allies against another similarly alien. Edmonds's focus remains always on "The Captives," and his novel is neither pro-Indian or anti-Indian; rather, like James Fenimore Cooper, he delineates the passing of the frontier—an earlier frontier than Cooper's—by giving his readers something of the effect that passing has on the people most involved in it.

In *Wilderness Clearing* Edmonds focuses upon the activities of the Destructives, his use of a contemporary term for the Indians, in the Mohawk Valley at the opening of the American Revolution. The story centers on two families who live across a ford from one another in a wilderness farming area on Black Creek, somewhere west of Little Falls, New York. The wilderness clearing of the title is, more specifically, that of Robert Gordon and his teenage daughter, Maggie. It is primeval American landscape, home to pioneering families in colonial York State.

> The wilderness imprisoned the clearing in a green silence. There was no cloud, no wind, not even a stirring of air. The water in Black Creek seemed sluggish; on the rift beside the mill its voice

was muted. The conical hills upon the barren, black-moss uplands stood as still as graveyard stones against the sky. [P. 1]

The author's depiction at the outset portrays the upstate settler's form before the Tories and the Indians set fire to the house and drive out the homesteaders.

This, on the first of August 1777, was Robert Gordon's place. No living sign of man or beast was visible on it anywhere. It remained so all through the day, until the sun, swinging westward, cast slanting arrowlike shadows through the stems of the wheat. By then the heat haze had moved down from the northern hills and the sun, shining through it, had taken shape. Way off in the woods a woodpecker started drilling on a tree.

The bird had been at work only a short time when another sound entered the silence from the north. This was the slow uncertain clank of a cowbell. But it steadily approached through the woods towards the ford over Black Creek that led to Mount's place. A nondescript cow, limp-eared, and amiable, dawdled into the open and down to the creek, to which she dropped her muzzle. [P. 2]

Such is the domestic scene at the wheat raiser's house in the Mohawk Valley wilderness. This book follows closely the rather simple yet extremely eventful comings and goings into the wilderness clearing of the Gordon's, as York State prepares to face the emerging war that engulfs the entire country. It is also, like numerous other Edmonds stories, the depicting of an emerging maturity, in this case of Maggie Gordon's neighbor Dick Mount, only a shade under Maggie's own age and therefore just a boy to the frontier girl-become-woman. In a natural way Maggie comes around, like Ernest Hemingway's Robert Wilson, to a recognition that maturity is not a matter of one's birthday. "I don't think how old a person is," she finally admits, "has anything to do with what he really is himself" (p. 132).

Adam Dingman, as the American ranger assigned to patrol the wilderness, and Tory sympathizers among the Fairfield men who run with the Indians play their various roles in this tale, which rambles on, its gait pitched to that of frontier living itself. The anguish and travail, to say nothing of the sheer determination, like that of a Hamlin Garland character, that exists simply because it *has* to, are captured by Edmonds as Maggie and Dick Mount face the coming of

the Destructives, afraid, alone, in the wilderness where every noise—
or silence—suddenly takes on a new and furtive meaning. *Wilderness Clearing* is an episode in the history of York State during the
Revolution, an episode concerning but a very few people, but their
sustained determination and pragmatic maturity, as Edmonds depicts them, contributed substantially to the future United States of
America. Furthermore, *Wilderness Clearing* exemplifies Thomas
Paine's message to the fighting colonials in *The American Crisis,*
when he accepted the war not because he disliked peace but because
he preferred war in his day to a postponement that would engulf his
children. At the very close of the story, Maggie wants to know if
Dick Mount wouldn't really rather go back to Jerseyfield, which
seems more secure and untouched by war. "I don't know if I want to
go back there," Dick said. "There's better farming land. But I don't
want to get chased away from here. If everybody started clearing
out, pretty soon it wouldn't be safe even in Jersey. I want to stick
around until it's safe even for kids like George and Henry to be left
alone on any farm that's mine or anybody else's" (p. 156).

NORTH AND SOUTH: *CADMUS HENRY*

In its theme of the interdependence of human beings, *Cadmus
Henry,* also published in 1949, is similar to *Wilderness Clearing.* It
tells the story of a southern youth during the Civil War who joined
General Bankhead Magruder's staff as clerk in the adjutant's office.
Bored with sitting out the war drafting reports and directives, he
volunteers for an observer's job with General Johnston's headquar-
ters, only to find out that an "observer" made him a Confederate
"aeronaut" looking at northern troop movements from a hot air former show balloon, the *Pizzini,* uncomfortably trying to avoid enemy
fire. After an initial sortie he would have quit, but Cadmus Henry
"was stuck with the balloon job tighter than a tick in a sheep's ear"
(p. 41). When the balloon got away from its moorings, his real experiences began. A southern girl, whose brother was in the 21st Massachusetts Regiment, rescues Cadmus from the York River, into which
his balloon had descended, and the fallen aeronaut gets a dry coat in-
tended for a fugitive slave. Puzzled by her northern, abolitionist

sympathies, and puzzled even more by the lack of logic in her failure to apply them rigidly, Cadmus admitted his failure to understand.

> "I don't see why you helped me then."
> "I wouldn't let a white man drown, any more than I would a Negro," she said. [P. 91]

Later he remembered her kindness, and "it didn't seem to matter that he knew she wanted the Union to win, though he knew that it ought to" (p. 94). As Cadmus fumbled for words to express his feeling to his Great Uncle Eppa, he had difficulty conveying his conflict. A balloonist's-eye view of things gave a different perspective somehow. He liked General Magruder well enough, he said, and it wasn't just that he was tired of writing out "high-sounding orders."

> . . . and yet, when you saw the two lines set one close against the other, they looked pretty much the same, and from that high part of the sky you might have had the armies shifted without seeing any real difference; and there didn't seem much purpose in what the generals did with their moving regiments and brigades here and there and making bold lines on their maps that ordinary men had to whittle out of the raw face of the earth with their sweat and aching backs. Cadmus said when he started his ballooning he'd hoped it was going to mean a commission for him, because he knew it would please his folks. He felt that way when he was coming back, before he had reported in to General Johnston. But now he wasn't sure he felt that way at all. He didn't know what had changed him. Maybe it was meeting the girl with the slaves, or maybe because nobody seemed to care what happened to a balloonist, once his balloon was gone. He didn't know, but he had the feeling that the real people in the army were the people who carved the work out in the lines and did the marching and got shot at if necessary. [Pp. 125–26]

"I think I understand the way you feel," he was told. A corollary action in this short novel is the loyalty of the two Negroes, Mebane and Mink, who took charge of Cadmus Henry's horse, a valued parting gift from his Great Uncle Eppa, while the youth was ballooning; and who, after Cadmus Henry was presumed lost, returned the animal to his home at great personal risk to themselves. In his whole military experience "he had found no truer friends than these two Negroes" (p. 134). Like Huckleberry Finn, Cadmus Henry had learned that humanity is not one side or another, nor is it one color or another.

CHILDREN'S BOOKS

It is difficult to classify a number of Edmonds's shorter works. Although technically speaking *Wilderness Clearing* and *Cadmus Henry* belong to the category of books for high-school readers, they are by no means limited in their appeal for adults. To the list it would be important to add, also, at least in passing, Edmonds's *Mr. Bendict's Lion* (1950), a light-hearted story of the misadventures of an English instructor at Miss Saterlee's Female Seminary; his *Corporal Bess* (1952), which the *New Yorker* called "a superlative dog story"[4]; and *Bert Breen's Barn* (1975), which won Edmonds a National Book Award. Works like these were published, to use the publisher's occasional expression, as "young novels"; but the ordinary distinctions between books for young readers and books for adults Walter Edmonds has refused to allow. The basic elements, he insists, are the same: "The characters are exact, true to themselves, and maturely realized."[5]

When asked some years ago to submit an autobiographic statement for a reference book on junior authors, Edmonds replied that he felt his presence in a book of children's authors highly anomalous: "I have never written a book for children," he said. "My stories published as such were all originally written for adults and for the most part saw print in adult magazines."[6] In this way a number of his previously published short stories, mainly from the pages of the *Saturday Evening Post,* subsequently came out in volume form. In addition to *The Matchlock Gun* which won him his first children's book award in 1941, these include *Tom Whipple* (1942), *Two Logs Crossing* (1945), *Hound Dog Moses and the Promised Land* (1954), *Uncle Ben's Whale* (1955), and *They Had a Horse* (1962). Edmonds's insistence that such books were "never written down: they are only made simple"[7] illustrates his basic position about such editions for younger readers. The "faint decalcomania that is all prettyfied surface"[8] he could not admit for any serious reader. In these stories, then, as well as in the novelettes discussed earlier, he demonstrates versatility. Though they range widely, from the historical frontier with its individual determination in the face of warfare and other travails to the frantic concerns of a modern schoolteacher with a lion on his hands, Edmonds remained true to his objective. A linking factor among all these works—whether novelette, young novel, or children's book—has been artistic honesty.

When the National Institute of Arts and Letters announced Walter D. Edmonds's *Bert Breen's Barn* among the winners of the 1975 National Book Awards, it was appropriate in many ways. It was testimony especially that Edmonds, having gone through a twelve-year dry period, was writing, and publishing, critically recognizable work again at a fair clip. *Time To Go House* (1969), *Wolf Hunt* (1970), *Beaver Valley* (1971), and *The Story of Richard Storm* (1974) all came out within a very short period; also they were all "children's books," a new departure in the sense that Edmonds's previous books for young readers, as mentioned above, were book editions of earlier short stories published for adult readers.

Time To Go House was written about his beloved "Northlands" farm for his grandchildren. He read it to them in three evenings, he told a Utica newspaperman, and it was great fun.[9] The story of this young reader's novelette began in his mind, he says, some years before when he happened to be alone with his white Labrador at the farm in Boonville. "I had put the dog out and was standing in the moonlit hall when I saw two house mice playing the stair game. They and all the other animals in the story, including the Rockendollar rats, the coon, the bear, I saw face to face at one time or another and their actions in the story are all based on observation."[10]

As the story of *Time To Go House* opens, Smalleata the field mouse has found a red leaf, tumbling down from a tree. She turns to her Uncle Stilton, whom she greatly admires. He was very old and slightly portly, as Edmonds describes him; but Smalleata was sure that he knew everything there was to know.

> "But what does it mean, when the leaves turn red?" she asked.
> "Some leaves turn yellow and some turn orange," said Uncle Stilton as if that ended the subject. He was irritated at having his afternoon nap interrupted, but he was very fond of his young niece, whom he considered not only pretty but lively and sweet-natured. So he said more pleasantly, "What does it mean? Why, it means that it will soon be time to go house."
> "What's that?" asked Smalleata, who had never heard the phrase before, "How do you go house?"

"You are full of questions," Uncle Stilton said grumpily. But after a minute he recalled that Smalleata was a very young mouse, three months old to be exact, and therefore could not be expected to know such things. Indeed, it was to her credit that she wanted to learn, and that being so, she had certainly come to the right person for information. He would tell her.

"All the better class of mouse go house in the winter," he began somewhat pompously, and then remembered that of course Smalleata had no idea of what he meant by *winter*. "Winter is when it gets very cold and the field gets covered by snow, and when that happens the human people in the big house go away. They go away every winter and leave the house empty. That," he said significantly, "is when we mice move in." [Pp. 4–5]

Time To Go House is the story of Smalleata and her Grand Uncle Stilton and the rest of their family as they "go house," facing an assortment of perils from Honeysuckle, the bear; Reagan Ready, the fox; and Lennox, the cat. Interspersed in the story are typical Edmonds ingredients of gentle satire on human foibles and customs and political shenanigans. When the mice watch a television show in which the president of the United States, Abraham Lyndon, gives his State of the Human Union address, talking of a war between people in the northern half of a country far away fighting the people in the southern half, and of wheat that somehow can't be used to feed starving children in Mississippi ("Wherever that is!" thinks Smalleata), Edmonds's "mouse philosophy" makes its point. "Uncle Wensleydale could not understand why all the masses of wheat had to be stored only where the wheat fields were," says the author. "Why shouldn't there be grain elevators in the states that were usually short of food, where the poor people could get at them?" (p. 127). Later, Smalleata thought sleepily of the first TV show she had seen, and "the tired, sad Abraham Lyndon who was President of the Human Union, talking about his foolish war."

As Smalleata snuggled down in her new nest, she felt good. She was glad to be a mouse.

In *Wolf Hunt* Edmonds returned to colonial days. The setting for this novelette is the great bend of the Delaware, when in the summer of 1784 the stumped-toed wolf began attacking the flocks. Edmonds explains that he derived his story from an earlier account in Jay Gould's *History of Delaware County* (1856) of a wolf who had lost three toes of his forefoot.

For *Beaver Valley,* his next young person's novelette, Edmonds wrote another mouse story. In this one Skeet and his grand-father, Overdare, "an old deer mouse with no liking for beaver," speak out against the destruction both imminent and ecological as a colony of beavers settle in Skeet's peaceful valley and begin con-structing a series of dams. The parallel between these "eager bea-vers" of wildlife lore and human tract developers is not hard to find.

With *Bert Breen's Barn*, a book for older youngsters, Ed-monds fully utilized his native Boonville area for story and setting. Even more than that, the characters are vintage Edmonds. It is once again the Edmonds of "Honor of the County" and *The Boyds of Black River*.

The novel centers on young Tom Dolan, a North Country youth. His mother, Polly Ann (Hannaberry) Dolan, had named Tom after her mother's brother, who had been the only successful member of the family she had ever heard about, both sides. "He had a grocery store and had risen to become a justice of the peace. Not many fami-lies could boast of a relative like that and Polly Ann hoped that nam-ing her son for this great uncle might put the boy on the road to higher things" (pp. 6–7).

Polly Ann was one of five children—all daughters—of Chick Hannaberry, a widowed loafer who went fishing and hunting while his young 'uns scoured the hills and thickets for berries to sell to neighbor folk or in town. Polly Ann's marriage to Nob Dolan lasted five years—until he took off, leaving her alone to raise Tom and two younger sisters, the twins Cissie-Mae and Ellie. Polly Ann took in wash—or went to the townfolks' homes to do theirs—and, of course, she managed by berrying and milking.

By the time Tom Dolan was nine, he began to think he might help more, and he discussed his thoughts with Birdy Morris, an old man who kept a bare farm near Buck's Corners and eked a living from a few farm animals and money he earned mowing hay for those who didn't have their own rigs. Birdy had shown Tom where to fish and how to snare rabbits in winter. Tom learned a lot from the old man, in whom he confided his desire to patch up his mother's farm and perhaps get a better barn for themselves. In Tom's thirteenth summer Birdy invited him to take a look at the Widow Breen's barn over in the sand flats beyond Hawkinsville. Birdy had helped Bert Breen build that barn, and he was more than a mite proud of it.

> The barn was at the foot of the hill, facing the house. If the mow doors had been open someone sitting on the porch could have

Artist's rendering of "Bert Breen's Barn." Illustration by Wendell Minor, reproduced by permission of the artist.

looked straight through to the far end. Like most back country barns of the time, it had no clapboards and the unpainted siding showed daylight through the vertical cracks between the boards, which meant that there was no hay in the mow.

Birdy drove around the front of the barn to the far side where there was some shade to leave the horses in. They got down from the wagon and came back to the front of the barn and Birdy rolled the wide door back along its track. Inside it was cool and empty, and Tom could tell there hadn't been any animals in it for a good many years. You couldn't smell cow, though there were eight stanchions—the old-fashioned wooden kind—on each side of the run. The run itself was made of timber, pieces of six-by-six fitted close, making a smooth walkway. At the far end were two horse stalls. All the stabling was made snug with an inside wall of matched boarding. He could see it had been a comfortable barn for beasts, comfortable for a man to work in.

They went up the open steps in the corner opposite the horse stalls and Tom looked up from the mow floor with its layer of dusty chaff. There was a lot more room than he had guessed, seeing the barn from the outside. There were two bents between the ends and he could tell that they had been built right. They stood plumb and square, the cross timbers tenoned and pinned and a top truss to carry the purlins. They had all been sawed on two sides. The rafters were round spruce poles, carefully matched; but he expected their top sides had been sawed, too, to accommodate the roof boards. It looked to him as sound as it must have been the day it was built, and he began thinking how it would be if he could buy it and move it down to their own place by the river below Fisk Bridge.

He knew, though, there wasn't any sense in thinking of it. He didn't have any money at all. None of his family had any. Just the same he knew exactly where he would set it up if he did have it. But that was crazy too. How was a kid going to move those timbers down seven miles of road? Let alone taking them apart or putting them up again if it came to that? [Pp. 16–17]

With this introduction Edmonds has firmly laid the ground-work for his novel, for from that day on, all Tom Dolan could think of was owning the Breen barn. Leaving school, he managed to get a job at the Ackerman and Hook feed mill in Boonville at twenty-five cents a day. The walk from the Dolan farm was long and especially difficult in winter weather, but Tom was determined. Out of his wages, Ben Franklin-like, he gave his mother half for the house, and he saved up half against the time when he might have enough to make at least a down payment to the Widow Breen for the barn. But while his job at the feed mill prospered, Tom's plans for getting the barn didn't work out quite as smoothly as he anticipated. Even when the Widow Breen died, with the county likely to put the barn on the block for taxes if no relative showed up, Tom found he had to wait a while. The county, then, as it sometimes did if somebody offered a good price for the land, sold the Breen's twenty acres to Mr. Armond, whose thousand-acre estate bordered the Breen property on three sides. He didn't need the land, but the purchase would round off his property lines. The Armonds spent only the summers in Boonville, wintering in New York City. Disheartened but not discouraged, Tom decided to go directly to Mr. Armond to offer to buy the barn. And Billy-Bob Baxter, the lawyer, was probably right when he told Tom it was probably better this way anyway: he didn't really want the Breen's worthless land. "All it's worth is the barn that stands on it. And *that's* what you want," he had told Tom. "You'll be better off having just that" (p. 130).

Polly Ann took notice of Tom's state and told him not to worry so.

"You hadn't ought to get discouraged, Tom. Sure, it seems bigger than you thought, now you've learned what it means to get a thing done. But, Tom you got this idea about the Breen barn three years ago. You've never let go of it. You were a dreamy young boy then, and it seemed as long as you wished something it would surely be. Now you're sixteen. You've changed. You're big as some men are. Strong, too. And you've been growing up inside. But, Tom, that idea was good. It would be a sin to give it up because it looks some harder. That idea was what started you doing things, like working for Ackerman and Hook, like fixing up our house. It's not only been good for you, it's been so for the girls and me, and we are proud of you. You go and make Mr. Armond an offer, come spring."

She looked at him earnestly, searchingly, as she always did when she felt strongly about anything. He hoped suddenly that when he got married it might be to a girl who felt as earnest as Polly Ann did about things. It made him feel a good deal better about the barn then. And he thought back to what she had said once more the Sunday morning he made up his mind to drive over to see Armond. When he told Polly Ann where he was going, she took it as a matter of course. She smiled and wished him luck. [P. 137]

And so Tom Dolan bought the barn from Mr. Armond for $50 down (all he had saved up) and $25 to pay the next year; and with Birdy Morris' help began transferring the barn board by board to the Dolan's little place where he and Birdy had long since staked out just where it would go and how they'd do it.

How they did it fills out much of the rest of the story, the barn building climaxed by a barn raising that engages farm folk, townspeople from Boonville, and Tom's fellow feed mill hands in a memorable Sunday's work in the manner customary in an earlier America. At the same time, concerns over a possible treasure many thought old Bert Breen must have secreted on his farm and conflicts with the disreputable Flancher boys who bullied their way into a squatter's claim on the property to look for the near legendary treasure make the later chapters of the book highly adventurous storytelling.

Tom and his mother find the treasure, of course. In two chapters (49–50), their recovery of the Breen money becomes as fast paced and tension filled a story as any detective thriller. In this most recent work Edmonds proves to be still a master storyteller, a North Country yarnspinner. And the fact that it all happens over the canal tow path and in farmlands and villages adjacent to Boonville places it squarely with the earlier Edmonds fiction. Perhaps tongue-in-cheek, Edmonds can't resist a whimsical reference to his very first canal novel, *Rome Haul,* for the two horses Tom Dolan eventually buys in Utica from dealer Al Rathbun are named Dan and Molly, just like the two young people aboard the *Sarsey Sal!*

The day after discovering the treasure Tom Dolan has a real, honest-to-goodness bank account in Lambert's Boonville bank, with an entry for $9,240.00. More than that, of course, he has his barn finished. He has proved, like Tom Whipple, John Ames, Chad Hanna, and similar Edmonds youths, that an American lad, whether in the nineteenth century or the twentieth, can be anything he wants to, if he will only work with industry, optimism, and faith in himself.

8

"The Novelist's Sphere"

$\mathcal{W}$ ALTER D. EDMONDS HIMSELF OBSERVED, "You cannot generalize about writing."[1] The writer leaves his individual mark. Edmonds is no exception. He gained his inspiration, first of all, from his native state, New York, especially Boonville and the Black River Canal area of his youth; and, secondly, from Harvard College and Professor Charles Townsend Copeland of the Harvard English Department. Although he did experiment with different approaches to writing in the fiction the *Harvard Advocate* published during his undergraduate period, Edmonds has had little to do with formal methods of writing. He is more akin to the bards of old who sang their lyrical ballads that told of their personal experiences or of adventures they had heard about, each infused with a morality that knew right from wrong, courage from dishonor, and fashioned with the creative spontaneity of the true and talented artist.

In writing Edmonds draws upon many sources: from the unflagging memory of a North Country heritage filled with canal boats and farm adventures; from a remarkably cogent sense of American history; from a talent he himself modestly admits for storytelling; and, finally, from simply the need to create ordinary characters—people who are representative of common folk throughout history. His first book, *Rome Haul* in 1929, came without hesitation, without prodding: "a wonderful experience," he reported, for the book "seemed to write itself."[2] The second book, *The Big Barn*, took a bit more time, more effort. A third, he says, he threw away; but by 1940 Edmonds was an established short story writer, a novelist of growing popularity, and an author whose works had gone on to the Broadway theatre and motion pictures.

When Edmonds began writing, emphasis on the man-next-door and themes derived from within the United States were characteristic of the changing nature of American prose and of American writers' interests. The maturing of the short story, as editor Edward J. O'Brien referred to it in 1932,[3] had come about while Edmonds's career was getting under way; and if he was influenced by the literary trends of the times, brought about by Sherwood Anderson and other writers who followed Anderson's lead, he was—as one of the "new writers" the critics were speaking about—very probably also one of the shapers of the storytelling tradition in United States literature. So far as longer fiction was concerned, H. L. Mencken had commented in 1924 that the younger novelists were turning to America itself for inspiration, theme, subject. "These youngsters," he said, "are attempting a first-hand examination of the national scene, and making an effort to represent it in terms that are wholly American."[4] By 1930 Mencken's observation could very well have included Walter D. Edmonds.

HISTORY INTO LITERATURE: FACT, FOLKLORE, AND FICTION

The "American experience" underlies so much of Edmonds's writing that he seems at once philosopher and historian, as much as storyteller. Part and parcel of the American experience, the frontier is often a leading factor in his work, the books especially. In the frontier times of his part of the nation, Edmonds found ample subjects for his novels, sometimes his stories, and often his children's books. But whether focusing on Revolutionary era Mohawk Valley or the canal-building "West" of New York State in 1817, Edmonds is constantly examining the American experience, assessing and reassessing the values and validity of it, and showing the necessary relationship between the American ideal—"the Dream," as many have called it—and the people who have played, and continue to play, a part in making that ideal a reality. He seems always to be showing the need for continuing that ideal, for assuring its extension into the present day. Admittedly his literature for the most part deals with a simpler age, a less hectic past: but this focus allows the artist a certain vantage point. In Edmonds's fiction the necessary linkage between people and history is seen, and his feeling for people is rendered with engaging clarity. He is the best of patriots without being a flag-waver; he is the soundest of moralists without being an evangelist; and he is the ablest of teachers without being a pedant.

Edmonds the storyteller is also a very sound historical novelist; and his principal works, including his enduring 1936 novel *Drums Along the Mohawk*, are as authentic as history itself. Real people occupy his attention, and real people move in the virtual world of his fiction. As a historical novelist, he has always felt critical of the distortion in the writings of those authors who used the genre merely as a vehicle to provide "a good gallop on a romancer's knee," as he put it.[5] At the same time, he applauds the integrity of a novel like *The Trees* by his fellow craftsman Conrad Richter. "Nothing very grand happens in it," Edmonds wrote of Richter's novel, "but when you finish it you will have lived in its time."[6] Such novelists shed considerably more light on a narrow scene, such as the Mohawk Valley in the American Revolution in the case of Edmonds's *Drums Along the Mohawk*, than many historians do in their factually detailed and faithfully documentary writing. Similarly, Edmonds's historical fiction is significant, as one critic has said, "because he has concentrated on a time about which history can afford only to generalize. Mr. Edmonds has succeeded in giving it life, vitality, importance for its own sake."[7] One asks, of course, that the historical novelist or story writer be true to his history, which is not necessarily the same thing as sticking to the facts of it. The trained historian gives us the event, the action; and authors like Walter D. Edmonds can give us the *people* in the event or action, who are in the final analysis the real makers of history. In the doing, such a writer can produce literary art of a high order.

An important aspect of Edmonds's writing career has been his discovery for twentieth-century writers not only of an upstate New York in general but also of the times and lives of the canal era in particular. He stimulated the "new regionalism," and he sired the canal novel. Without a doubt, Edmonds has influenced many other authors toward New York State themes or settings; and in the case of the subgenre I have dubbed the canal novel, he certainly proved to be the literary progenitor of other writers' works. Notable among these are the several novels, *Canal Town* (1944), *Sunrise to Sunset*

(1950) and *Banner by the Wayside* (1947), of Samuel Hopkins Adams: all are set along the famous waterway that was New York's Erie Canal.[8]

The Erie Canal is Edmonds's Moby Dick, for it appears to be good and bad, at times a magnetic force drawing humanity toward it and into its influence as into a vortex, at other times repelling them. Like the great, enigmatic whale of Herman Melville, the novelist who lived for a time in Albany, New York, and wrote into his *Moby Dick* (1851) a chapter on canallers, the Erie Canal is the greatest of its species.[9]

Edmonds's real heroes may at times not be individual persons as in the conventional novel at all, but rather people in general; or canals, barns, and circuses around which the common folk lived and worked. Besides the obvious frontiersmen in such colonial period works as *Drums Along the Mohawk* and *In the Hands of the Senecas,* many other characters who people his fiction are, in a quite real sense, frontier folk—close to the soil, to the canal boat, or to the circus with which and for which they strive for a livelihood. The lock tender, for example, on the old Erie Canal or the Black River Canal was as much a pioneer and frontiersman in his way as were Daniel Boone and his counterparts as settlers in Tennessee or the western territories of the country. Edmonds's prose style, too, is liberally sprinkled with proverbial comparisons and down-to-earth similes which comprised much of the everyday vernacular of earlier times. It seems organically related to an essentially frontier culture about which he writes.

Certainly a basic characteristic of Edmonds's novels and stories is a reliance upon native-set humor. This, too, is tied to a frontier type culture and is an integral part of Edmonds's overall historical emphasis; as a writer, he shows an uncommonly firm grasp of the American frontier, both in his locality and in general of the mores of early American life. He is a modern literary descendant, too, of the frontier humorist; and his mastery of style, with its controlled ironic deflation, is comparable to that of Twain. Edmonds's famous racing caterpillar, "Red Peril," whether akin to Clemens's equally well-known Calaveras County jumping frog or not, and tales like those of the Black Maria, the itching bear, or the "cashalot" whale on a canal boat are just as authentic and mirthful Americana.[10] Edmonds's involvement in folklore was a natural occurrence. As he listened to old canallers' yarns, he grew up close to one of the well-defined subcultures of New York State. He was not only reared in canal lore and farm life as he experienced them at Northlands and along the Black River Valley but also was imbued with a North Country appreciation of the folk hero and tall tale of Paul Bunyan tradition. The preposterousness of "The Itching Bear" story, which appeared in *The Forum*, June 1930, fades as the plausibility of the tale—artfully and patiently built, just as in that long-before story of "Black Maria" in the *Harvard Advocate*—takes over in the reader's mind. The reader of "The Itching Bear" is being told a folk tale, a tall tale, one of hundreds upon hundreds that have come out of the vast Adirondack hills. It becomes a paradox of utter absurdity versus it-might-have-happened, and the telling yields a memorable vignette of fiction. In Edmonds's art a fearsome black bear can be reduced to a humorous if frightfully momentous adversary for a North Country lad; a dead whale can make a trip over the historic Erie Canal, a circus troupe can make money by exhibiting "the only dead lion in captivity"; or an English professor can somehow manage to forego buying the new pianoforte his girl seminary students need and wind up with a Madagascan lion instead. In such tales the chuckles of the readers indicate their mirthful accepting of the incredible: as with all good storytellers, Edmonds has us believing.

In keeping with the frontier sensibility which so often can be found in his fiction, both novel and story, Edmonds frequently has given his leading figures overtly symbolic names—Rose Wilder, Dan Harrow, Young Ames, for instance—that further tie them to the cultural setting (whether agricultural, canal, or mercantile) and the times of early America. Common to a number of Edmonds's novels is the young person who finds his maturity not only through ordinary growth and experience but also, importantly, in and through the times of the country's expansion. These figures—especially Chad Hanna, Jerry Fowler in *Erie Water*, Dan Harrow in *Rome Haul*, and John Ames in *Young Ames*—symbolize young America in the first half of the nineteenth century. So, also, do Tom Whipple and other youths in the short stories. In their diverse ways and settings they are all striving in a developing cultural milieu that is basically frontier in orientation. Through such characters Edmonds suggests the need for a continuous re-evaluation of the national character and the individual's place in its formation, a re-evaluation which reminds his readers of the idealism, the morality, and spirit that are central to the "American Dream." Edmonds demonstrates again and again how close the ideal and the pragmatic are—and have always been—in the American experience, that the twin poles of the spiritual and the practical that Van Wyck Brooks delineated in 1915 are not really contradictory values. Without that idealism—the necessary spiritual center—the pragmatic and the practical become nothing more than mere expediency.

WOMEN AND MEN IN EDMONDS'S FICTION

In the earlier novels an Edmonds plot customarily required a sprawling landscape and a large cast of people; and the times and the people collectively often remain more memorable in an Edmonds novel than do particular individuals. In *Drums Along the Mohawk* one's attention focuses upon the average New York State farmer and his resistance not just to the Britain of George III but to the disruption of war itself. For *Rome Haul* and *Erie Water* this center-of-focus is the big-as-life canal and all its people, whether builders, boaters, or lock tenders. For *The Big Barn* the very title conveys the author's major emphasis; as fascinating as Ralph Wilder and other characters may be as individuals, the barn bulks larger still. For *Chad Hanna,* as indicated by Edmonds's perhaps more apt title, "Red Wheels Rolling," for the serialized version in the *Post,* the real focus is the circus and the day-to-day concerns engendered by the nomadic circus life typical of the traveling shows of the 1830s in rural America.

In every instance, however, the fact that the traditional hero is upstaged, as it were, by the vastness either of cast or setting does not preclude an analysis of Edmonds's characters as literary figures of more than incidental importance and interest. Many are carefully drawn and, especially in the case of those in historical settings, authentically depicted. His male characters are generally more fully developed and have considerably more importance than his women, partly one suspects because they are forever caught up in a man's world of constant physical struggle, whether for safety or livelihood.

Edmonds's women are far removed from romantic fiction's usual, tradition-bound stereotypes like William Dean Howells's Editha or A. E. W. Mason's Ethne; but at the same time one must confess to wanting something of the intellectual stamina that ought to accompany the practical, housewifery side of things, especially on the frontier. Considered collectively, Edmonds's women tend to exhibit a shallow intellectual nature, and the reader may find them pale and, like Editha or Ethne—for quite different reasons—rather boring. In his major works, to give specific examples, one finds little gumption and certainly no real assertiveness in Magdelana Borst (*Drums Along the Mohawk*), Caroline Trig (*Chad Hanna*), or Mary Fowler (*Erie Water*), even though they are married to, or otherwise closely linked with, the central male character in each book. Molly Larkins, of *Rome Haul,* may be a bit more independent throughout Edmonds's first novel than these other women are in theirs, yet even she is a relatively passive character. In the case of Christine Chevelier, whom John Ames is determined to woo and win in the novel *Young Ames,* we find the woman's part is essentially that of an off-stage character. All told, they appear relatively passionless.

There are some exceptions to the charge of the women characters' thin intellectuality, I hasten to add, for Rose Wilder (*The Big Barn*), Kathy O'Chelrie (*The Boyds of Black River*), and to a large extent Polly Ann Dolan (*Bert Breen's Barn*) show their mettle and exhibit an assertive self-confidence in their respective novels. Then, too, other exceptions exist, of course, depending upon the circumstances and times depicted, for there is nothing pale about Delia Borst, Caty Breen, or Martha Dygart as they endure captivity in *In the Hands of the Senecas*. Older women, it should further be noted, generally fare better in Edmonds's hands and have more substance than younger ones, as evidenced by Mrs. MacLennar (*Drums Along the Mohawk*), Ma Halleck (*Erie Water*), Mrs. Huguenine (*Chad Hanna*), and the Indian Newataquaah (*In the Hands of the Senecas*). All are active, forceful figures with a firm hand on life.

When one looks at Walter D. Edmonds's work as a whole, another common element runs through his fiction. A notable thematic similarity in several novels involves a young couple and the matron who befriends them. In this connection it is obvious that Edmonds sees mature women as essentially important and sagacious advisors or confidantes. Thus Jerry and Mary Fowler lean on Ma Halleck in *Erie Water;* Dan Harrow and Molly Larkins in *Rome Haul* find a confidante in Mrs. Gurget; and Chad Hanna and Caroline Trig turn to Mrs. Huguenine for advice and support in *Chad Hanna.* In Edmonds's shorter fiction, too, this pattern is also followed when, for example, in the story of "Big-Foot Sal," Edmonds uses the substitute mother figure as his primary focus.

It must be obvious to anyone who reads even a small amount of Edmonds's fiction that the author likes young 'uns—to use the Yorker expression for youths. Many of his stories, if not most of them, are those of youth. Frequently and significantly, his fiction centers on the twin themes of young people and a young country. Tom Whipple (in "Tom Whipple, the Acorn, and the Emperor of Russia") serves as his most engrossing example, typical of the Edmonds young lad hero. He is young in years and a bit naive, as is his country, but Tom Whipple's innate morality and his sense of personhood, as we would say today, engender respect in the tsar of Russia. When one is finished reading *Chad Hanna*, he feels that Chad will certainly make it: he will move forward as the nation moves westward, indicated by the closing dialogue in the novel. Cadmus Henry learns— and impresses upon the reader—the idiocy of warfare and the true meaning of brotherhood. And Yankee Yorker youth John Ames just about beats New York City's financial district at its own game, despite his tender age and inexperience. Tom Dolan, in *Bert Breen's Barn*, had a dream and stuck to it, despite all but insurmountable obstacles; he proved that an American lad can pretty well achieve whatever he wants if he will only work hard at it and have faith in the rightness of his effort. Persistence and initiative do pay off.

Other figures come to mind also: Teddy Armond, of "Honor of the County" and *The Boyds of Black River*, into which novel the story was incorporated; Trudy Van Alstyne of "The Spanish Gun"; and John Haskell in "Judge", to name a few others who represent youngsters the author admires. Whether from historical times or more recent periods, they have that quality of integrity, morality, and right mindedness, coupled with a pragmatic sense of what must be done, that engages the reader's attention, as well as his respect. Without being didactic in the least, Edmonds's depictions of such young people provide a balanced sense of history and a valid lesson for the present time as well.

Walter D. Edmonds is an uncompromising realist when it comes to old-fashioned morality, and an advocate of the American experience. He has always written responsibly on his own terms. "Some writers," he observed in an article for the *Atlantic Monthly*, "can tailor their talent to fit a particular market; but the work they produce will never be literature—at the best it will be only high-class

Walter D. Edmonds and his wife, Katharine, pause with their pet Jack Russell terrier, Erlo, on the footbridge at "Northlands," the Boonville farm where Edmonds was born. Photograph by Leo Hobaica, courtesy of the Utica *Observer Dispatch*.

dress goods."[11] What Edmonds has had to tell, he has had to tell truthfully, in his own way. There is probably no more sincere writer in contemporary letters than Edmonds. Whether in his major novels or in his shorter pieces, his expressed purpose has most often been the delineation of American history and the relation of that history to the present day. "What I want to show," he said, back when he accepted the Newbery Medal for his first children's book, "are the qualities of mind the spirit of plain ordinary people, who after all carry the burden of human progress. I want to know about people, how they loved, what they hoped for, what they feared."[12] Edmonds has underscored in several instances this essential buttress of his writing. He felt, he has said, that American writers, with the wit to tell it truly, have the greatest of stories to tell. It must be in terms of "doing and think and hoping" of the ordinary citizens, for this, he believes, "is the novelist's sphere."[13]

America and the Americans, Edmonds said, "are still, as it were, at the first beginning. We are just born, now, and I for one profoundly feel we are just beginning to see."[14] When he writes historical fiction, there is an air of uncompromising sincerity and validity about it. When he creates simple folk in comic situations, there is an air of honest mirth unalloyed. When he spins a tale of children, he speaks at the same time to the hearts and minds of parents.

Walter D. Edmonds has always conveyed in his writing, from major novel or short story to novelettes and books for young readers, the necessary but happy balance between taking the world seriously and feeling the *joie de vivre* that must also be found for life to have its fullest meaning. From Lana Martin's peacock feather to Tom Whipple's acorn, with Edmonds perspective is essential.

Notes

WHERE THE PAGE NUMBERS are cited in the text following a quoted passage, they refer to the first book edition as listed in the Bibliography. Page citations are not given for material quoted from magazines, as the Bibliography provides the original publication data for each story.

1—BACKGROUND FOR A WRITER

1. Walter D. Edmonds, *Two Logs Crossing: John Haskell's Story* (New York: Dodd, Mead, 1945).

2. Richard Benedetto, "Spinner of Yarns Knits Novels of Our Rich Regional Heritage," *Sunday Observer-Dispatch* (Utica, N.Y.), July 14, 1974.

3. Howard Thomas, *Black River in the North Country* (Prospect, N.Y.: Prospect Books, 1963), p. 5.

4. Carl Carmer, "Walter Edmonds of Black River Valley," *Publisher's Weekly* 151 (June 27, 1942): 2346.

5. Walter D. Edmonds, quoted in "Walter Dumaux Edmonds," in Muriel Fuller, ed., *More Junior Authors* (New York: H. W. Wilson, 1963), p. 73.

6. This was especially true for *Rome Haul*, his first novel. Walter D. Edmonds, letter to author, February 1959.

7. Benedetto, "Spinner of Yarns."

8. Richard H. Costa, *Edmund Wilson: Our Neighbor from Talcottville* (Syracuse, N.Y.: Syracuse University Press, 1980), pp. 126–27.

9. Walter D. Edmonds, letter to author (August 1981).

10. David McCord, "Edmonds Country," *Saturday Review of Literature* 17 (December 11, 1927): 10.

11. See Walter D. Edmonds, *The Big Barn* (Boston: Little, Brown, 1930), pp. 40, 46.

12. Walter D. Edmonds, in *Newbery Medal Books: 1922-1955,* Horn Book Papers, 1 (Boston: The Horn Book, 1955): 210.

13. The Choate School (C. V. Pierce), letter to author (August 1964).

14. "Walter D. Edmonds," *Wilson Bulletin* 4 (November 1929): 26.

15. David McCord, "Edmonds Country," p. 10.

16. J. Donald Adams, *Copey of Harvard: A Biography of Charles Townsend Copeland* (Boston: Houghton Mifflin, 1960), p. 175.

17. Ibid.

18. Ibid.

2—APPRENTICESHIP AT HARVARD

1. *Newbery Medal Books: 1922-1955,* Horn Book Papers, 1 (Boston: The Horn Book, 1955): 210.

2. See *Harvard Advocate Catalog 1866-1938* (Cambridge, Mass.: Harvard University, 1938).

3. Walter D. Edmonds, letter to author (February 1959).

4. Charles Grayson, ed., *Stories for Men: An Anthology* (Garden City, N.Y.: Garden City Publishing Co., 1944), p. 137.

5. See Walter D. Edmonds, "The Hind Quarters of an Elephant," *Harvard Advocate* 112 (September 1925): 35-37.

6. Leslie Reed, *The Rector of Maliseet* (New York: E. P. Dutton, 1925), see *Harvard Advocate* 112 (October 1925): 60-61.

7. Walter D. Edmonds, "Up-River Mists and Lilacs," *Harvard Advocate* 110 (March 1, 1924): 244.

8. Walter D. Edmonds, "'Jehu,'" *Harvard Advocate* 108 (January 1, 1922): 106. This early college submission describing a village fair in upstate New York bears comparison with the author's later description of a circus show in the village of Canastota, New York, in *Chad Hanna,* his 1940 novel. See Walter D. Edmonds, *Chad Hanna* (Boston: Little, Brown, 1940), pp. 110-111, and below, Chapter 6.

9. During the term of Edmonds's presidency of the *Advocate,* Copeland became Boylston Professor of Rhetoric and Oratory at Harvard. An editorial in the *Advocate* for March 1925, when Edmonds was president-elect, pointed to Copey as "one of the few inspirational teachers left to Harvard."

10. David McCord, "Edmonds Country," *Saturday Review of Literature* 17, no. 7 (December 11, 1937): 11.

11. Walter D. Edmonds, letter to author (February 1959). When the story appeared, Edmonds points out, *Scribner's Magazine* also included the first published short story of one of his fellow students, "Extra! Extra!" by Robert E. Sherwood.

3—EDMONDS'S SHORT STORIES

1. Robert E. Spiller, *The Cycle of American Literature* (New York: Mentor, 1957), p. 162.

2. *U.S. Stories: Regional Stories from the Forty-Eight States,* selected with a foreword by Martha Foley and Abraham Rothberg (New York: Hendricks House-Farrar Straus, 1949), p. xv.

3. Edward J. O'Brien, ed., *Best Short Stories of 1932* (New York: Dodd, Mead, 1932), Introduction.

4. H. L. Mencken, *Prejudices: Fourth Series* (New York: Alfred A. Knopf, 1924), p. 283.

5. See Sculley Bradley, "Sherwood Anderson," in Sculley Bradley et al., eds., *The American Tradition in Literature,* rev. ed. (New York: Norton, 1961), 2: 1043; see Henry Seidel Canby, "Fiction Sums Up a Century," in Robert E. Spiller et al., eds., *Literary History of the United States,* rev. ed. (New York: Macmillan, 1960), p. 1233.

6. Canby, "Fiction Sums Up a Century," p. 1233.

7. Foley and Rothberg, *U.S. Stories,* p. xv.

8. Edward J. O'Brien, ed., *Best Short Stories of 1933* (New York: Dodd, Mead, 1933), p. xxii.

9. David McCord, "Edmonds Country," *Saturday Review of Literature* 17, no. 7 (December 11, 1937): 11.

10. Ellery Sedgwick, ed., *Atlantic Harvest* (Boston: Little, Brown, 1947), p. 421.

11. Canby, "Fiction Sums Up a Century," p. 1233.

12. Robert M. Gay, "The Historical Novel: Walter D. Edmonds," *Atlantic Monthly* 165 (May 1940): 657.

13. "The Cruise of the Cashalot" first appeared in *The Forum and Century* (January 1932) pp. 24–31. It was collected in Edmonds' *Mostly Canallers* (Boston: Little, Brown, 1934) and *Seven American Stories* (Boston: Little, Brown, 1970), and appeared in *O. Henry Memorial Award Prize Stories of 1932.* It also came out as a separate book for children under the title *Uncle Ben's Whale* (New York: Dodd, Mead, 1955).

14. See Edmonds's epilogue to Nathaniel R. Howell, "A Long Island Whale Story," *New York Folklore Quarterly* 10 (Spring 1954): 42–44.

15. Blanche Colton Williams, ed., *O. Henry Memorial Award Prize Stories of 1932* (Garden City, N.Y.: Doubleday, Doran, 1932), pp. xxiii–xxiv. Rudyard Kipling reportedly loved Bullen's book, calling it "immense—there is no other word" (ibid.). Bullen, who wrote thirteen books between 1898 and 1915, sailed on the *Cachalot* out of New Bedford, Massachusetts, at the age of eighteen.

16. See A. M. Drummond and Robert E. Gard, *The Cardiff Giant* (Ithaca, N.Y.: Cornell University Press, 1949). Included in the book, along with the regional play of the title, is Andrew D. White's factual essay on the Cardiff Giant affair.

17. "Contributor's Column," *Atlantic Monthly* 143 (March 1929): 429.

18. For the cholera see Samuel Hopkins Adams, "Our Forefathers Tackled an Epidemy—the Cholera of 1832," *New York Folklore Quarterly* 3, no. 2 (Summer 1947): 93-101; and Adams' short story, "The Monster of Epidemy," in his *Grandfather Stories* (New York: Random House, 1955), pp. 57-69.

19. See Lionel D. Wyld, "The Quadrupedal Sam Adams," *Hamilton Alumni Review* 29 (Summer 1964): 4-8.

20. "Finis Wilson (God rest him) was an actual man," Edmonds wrote, "and no greater than I have attempted to depict him," "Contributor's Column," p. 429.

21. From a song sung by Cork Leg Jonny Bartley in Buffalo's Bonny's Theatre in the 1870s; see John A. and Alan Lomax, *American Ballads and Folk Songs* (New York: Macmillan, 1934), p. 463.

22. Walter D. Edmonds, "Author's Note," *Saturday Evening Post* 210 (July 17, 1937): 41. This story later earned Edmonds the Newbery Medal when it was published separately as a small book, *The Matchlock Gun* (1941).

23. *Jubilee: One Hundred Years of the Atlantic*, sel. and ed. Edward Weeks and Emily Flint (Boston: Little, Brown, 1957), pp. 439-43. "Moses" initially appeared in the August 1938 *Atlantic Monthly;* it was published separately as a book under the title *Hound Dog Moses and the Promised Land* (New York: Dodd, Mead, 1954).

24. "Honor of the County" was incorporated into the novel *The Boyds of Black River* (1953); the stories about the Ames youth formed the basis for a novel by the same name: *Young Ames* (1942). Both of these works are discussed more fully in Chapter 6.

25. *Saturday Evening Post* 208 (July 27, 1935): 76. "Judge" was reprinted in *Post Stories of 1935)* (Boston: Little, Brown, 1936).

26. Walter D. Edmonds, *Two Logs Crossing* (New York: Dodd, Mead, 1945), Foreword.

4—*ROME HAUL* AND THE CANAL NOVEL

1. Quoted in David McCord, "Edmonds Country," *Saturday Review of Literature* 17, no. 7 (December 11, 1937): 11.

2. Samuel Hopkins Adams, *Grandfather Stories* (New York: Random House, 1955), p. 96.

3. Walter D. Edmonds, letter to author (February 1959).

4. Walter D. Edmonds, *Rome Haul* (New York: Modern Library, 1938), pp. viii-ix.

5. *New York Herald Tribune Books,* February 17, 1929, p. 5.

6. Actually the first Erie novel was a juvenile book, *Marco Paul's Travels and Adventures in the Pursuit of Knowledge on the Erie Canal,* written by Jacob Abbott and published in 1844 (Boston: T. H. Carter & Co., and New York: A. V. Blake); see Lionel D. Wyld, *Low Bridge! Folklore and the Erie Canal* (Syracuse, N.Y.: Syracuse University Press, 1977), pp. 127-28.

7. Walter D. Edmonds, letter to author (February 1959). The Harlow book Edmonds refers to is a classic among canal buffs: Alvin F. Harlow, *Old Towpaths: The Story of the American Canal Era* (New York and London: D. Appleton, 1926).

8. For a glossary of canal argot, see Lionel D. Wyld, "A Yorker Dictionary of Canalese," in *The Erie Canal: Gateway to Empire,* ed. Barbara K. and Warren S. Walker (Boston: D. C. Heath, 1963), pp. 97–102.

9. For a more extended treatment, see Lionel D. Wyld "Canallers in Waste Land: Some Considerations of Edmonds' *Rome Haul,*" *Midwest Quarterly* 4, no. 4 (Summer 1963): 335–41.

10. "Following the enthusiastic reception by critics and public alike of Walter D. Edmonds's first novel, *Rome Haul,* in April 1929," wrote Thomas F. O'Donnell, "various aspects of life in upstate New York became grist for the mills of other writers who quickly appeared to follow, deliberately or not, Edmonds' successful example of the new regionalism. Whereas the decade before *Rome Haul* had produced a scant half dozen novels in which the great upstate area provides an identifiable, significant background, the decade that followed . . . produced at least three dozen. The next decade, the 1940s, saw the publication of at least sixty more. And during the first half of . . . the 1950s, there have been at least fifty," Thomas F. O'Donnell, "The Regional Fiction of Upstate New York" (Ph.D. Diss., Syracuse University, 1957), pp. 5–6).

11. Iowa City *Press Citizen,* September 29, 1932. Elser's play appears in G. H. Leverton, ed., *Plays for a College Theater* (New York: Samuel French, 1932).

12. *The Daily Northwestern* (Evanston, Illinois), October 20, 1932. Lee Mitchell, who later became chairman of the Department of Theatre at Northwestern University, designed the settings for *Low Bridge.*

13. Iowa City *Press Citizen,* September 29, 1932. *Low Bridge* shared the series with new plays by such playwrights as Lynn Riggs (who directed his own play for the University Theatre), E. P. Conkle, Virgil Geddes, Paul Green, and Maxwell Anderson.

14. *Fonda: My Life as Told to Howard Teichmann* (New York and Scarborough, Ont.: New American Library, 1981), p. 89.

15. Ibid., pp. 89–90.

16. Walter D. Edmonds, letter to author (December 1981).

17. *Theatre Arts Monthly* 18 (December, 1934): 902–903.

18. See Burns Mantle, ed., *The Best Plays of 1934–1935* (New York: Dodd, Mead, 1935).

19. *Theatre Arts Monthly,* p. 903.

20. For this viewpoint I am happy to acknowledge the work of Bernice Bauemler, who prepared under my direction at State University of New York at Buffalo a graduate paper, "The Novel, the Real Drama," in which she compared the three works.

21. Howard Thomas, *Black River in the North Country* (Prospect, N.Y.: Prospect Books, 1963), p. 178.

22. Robert M. Gay, "The Historical Novel: Walter D. Edmonds," *Atlantic Monthly* 165 (May 1940): 657. Gay called Ralph Wilder Edmonds' "most ambitious portrait."

23. Librarian Walter Pilkington, Hamilton College, letter to author (February 1970).

24. Philip Freneau, "Stanzas on the Great Western Canal of the State of New York," New Brunswick (N.J.) *Fredonian*, August 8, 1822.

25. Walter D. Edmonds, *Rome Haul* (New York: Modern Library, 1936), p. x.

26. *Springfield* (Mass.) *Republican*, February 12, 1933.

5—*DRUMS ALONG THE MOHAWK*

1. Walter D. Edmonds, "How You Begin a Novel," *Atlantic Monthly* 158 (August 1938): 189.

2. Little, Brown and Company (N. L. Barr), letter to author (April 1964).

3. Edward Weeks's review appeared in the *Atlantic* for August 1936; that of Allan Nevins was in the *Saturday Review of Literature*, August 1, 1936.

4. "Walter D. Edmonds," in *Cyclopedia of World Authors*, ed. Frank N. Magill (New York: Salem Press, 1958), p. 329.

5. Richard G. Case, "'Drums' Author Going Strong," *Syracuse* (N.Y.) *Herald-American*, July 18, 1976.

6. Letter from Little, Brown and Company, as cited.

7. Walter D. Edmonds, *Drums Along the Mohawk* (Boston: Little, Brown, 1936), p. vii.

8. Edward Weeks, *In Friendly Candor* (Boston: Little, Brown, 1959), p. 81.

9. Edmonds, "How You Begin a Novel," p. 190.

10. "The Peacock's Feather" is the subject of the first part of Chapter 2; see Walter D. Edmonds, *Drums Along the Mohawk* (Boston: Little, Brown, 1936), pp. 20ff.

11. Edmonds, *Drums Along the Mohawk*, p. vii.

12. Robert M. Gay, "The Historical Novel: Walter D. Edmonds," *Atlantic Monthly* 165, no. 5 (May 1940): 657.

13. Walter D. Edmonds, "A Novelist Takes Stock," *Atlantic Monthly* 172 (July 1943): 76.

14. Ibid.

15. Ibid., p. 77.

6—UPSTATE, DOWNSTATE

1. Rose Fald, *Books* (April 7, 1970), p. 1.

2. Samuel Hopkins Adams, *Banner by the Wayside* (New York: Random House, 1947), p. 24.

3. H. A. Wooster, review in *Library Journal,* April 1, 1940; and R. Littell, review in *Yale Review* (Summer 1940).

4. Cf. the passage from "'Jehu,'" his first submission to the *Harvard Advocate,* as cited in Chapter 2.

5. When it serves the author's purpose to deal more specifically with the relationship between Negroes and whites, Edmonds does so. Note, for example, the feelings of Cadmus Henry toward the Negroes Mebane and Mink in his *Cadmus Henry* (New York: Dodd, Mead, 1949), p. 134.

6. The story "Big-Foot Sal" initially appeared in *Harper's Magazine* (December 1930), pp. 81–86; it was included in *Mostly Canallers.* Ma Halleck and Mrs. Gurget are characters in *Erie Water* (1933) and *Rome Haul* (1929), respectively.

7. C. Hartley Grattan, quoted in *O. Henry Memorial Award Prize Stories,* sel. and ed. Harry Hansen (Garden City: Doubleday, Doran, 1934), p. xiv. Grattan called it "by far the most effective story in the *Post* during the year covered."

7–SHORTER NOVELS AND CHILDREN'S BOOKS

1. Dayton Kohler, "Walter D. Edmonds: Regional Historian," *The English Journal* 27 (January 1938): 10.

2. Edmonds's Bella seems to have a literary kinship with Howells's Irene Lapham; and like her counterpart in *The Rise of Silas Lapham* Bella—plain in contrast to the more attractive sister—surprises the family by her marriage to a man everyone thought came courting her sister. It must be pointed out, however, that in Edmonds's story the situation is revealed to the reader only by Bella's reflecting upon past events and forms no essential part of the narrative as the similar facts do in the Howells novel.

3. W. A. MacDonald, review of *The Wedding Journey, New York Times,* October 12, 1947.

4. *New Yorker* 28 (December 6, 1952): 197.

5. Walter D. Edmonds, "Acceptance Paper," in *Newbery Medal Books: 1922-1955,* Horn Book Papers, 1 (Boston: The Horn Book, 1955): 221.

6. "Walter Dumaux Edmonds," in Muriel Fuller, ed., *More Junior Authors* (New York: H. W. Wilson, 1963), p. 73.

7. Edmonds, "Acceptance Paper," p. 73.

8. Ibid.

9. Richard Benedetto, "Spinner of Yarns Knits Novels of Our Rich Regional Heritage," *Sunday Observer-Dispatch* (Utica, N.Y.), July 14, 1974.

10. Walter D. Edmonds, from the dust jacket for *Time To Go House* (Boston: Little, Brown, 1969).

8–"THE NOVELIST'S SPHERE"

1. Walter D. Edmonds, "A Novelist Takes Stock," *Atlantic Monthly* 172 (July 1953): 73.

2. Ibid., p. 75.

3. Edward J. O'Brien, ed., *The Best Short Stories of 1932* (New York: Dodd, Mead, 1932), Introduction.

4. H. L. Mencken, *Prejudices: Fourth Series* (New York: Alfred A. Knopf, 1924), p. 283.

5. Edmonds, "A Novelist Takes Stock," p. 77. Edmonds was critical, for instance, of Hervey Allen's *The Forest and the Fort;* and he felt Kenneth Roberts's two novels, *Rabble in Arms* and *Arundel,* should not have been so casual in their use of history. He chides such writers for a lack of honest portrayal.

6. Ibid.

7. Arthur B. Tourtellot, "History and the Historical Novel," *Saturday Review of Literature* 22 (August 24, 1940): 4. A. T. Dickinson, Jr., *American Historical Fiction* (1958; 3rd ed., Metuchen, N.J.: Scarecrow Press, 1971) cites Tourtellot (p. 16) and calls attention to such Edmonds novels as *Drums Along the Mohawk* and *Wilderness Clearing* as works which "best evoke the spirit of frontier warfare" (p. 32).

8. See Lionel D. Wyld, "The Quadrupedal Sam Adams," *Hamilton Alumni Review* 29 (Summer 1964): 4–8, which summarizes the literary career of Adams. See also Lionel D. Wyld, "Adams: Rhapsodist of the Old Erie," *Low Bridge! Folklore and the Erie Canal* (Syracuse, N.Y.: Syracuse University Press, 1977), Chapter 10.

9. It is interesting to note that the couple whose home serves as a refuge for Jerry Fowler's wife in *Erie Water* is named Melville.

10. In commenting on the "Red Peril" story, Kenneth Payson Kempton observed that Edmonds "is rooted in reality." The story, he said, "is creative reporting lighted by satire at its best, at once amusing and instructive to all mankind," *Short Stories for Study* (Cambridge, Mass.: Harvard University Press, 1953), p. 114. Such a comment applies, of course, to more than just the caterpillar tale.

11. Edmonds, "A Novelist Takes Stock," p. 74.

12. Quoted in Dorothy M. Bryan, "Walter D. Edmonds, 1941 Newbery Winner," *Library Journal* 67 (July 1942): 602.

13. Walter D. Edmonds, "Acceptance Paper," in *Newbery Medal Books: 1922-1955,* Horn Book Papers, 1 (Boston: The Horn Book, 1955): 223.

14. Bryan, "Walter D. Edmonds," p. 603.

Bibliography

THIS BIBLIOGRAPHY includes no translated material, although one should be aware that Edmonds has been reprinted abroad, most notably his perennial bestseller, *Drums Along the Mohawk,* which appeared, for example, as *Die Schlacht in Mohawktal* (Berlin: Fischer, 1938). It presents material in English. In the case of Edmonds's numerous books, only the first (hardcover) publication is listed. Several of his novels have been available in paperback under the same titles given here; but in one case—that of *The Big Barn*—the reprint title was changed (to *The Magnificent Wilders*).

This primary materials bibliography contains all of the writer's *Harvard Advocate* fiction and other pieces published during his undergraduate days at Cambridge.

BOOKS

Rome Haul. Boston: Little, Brown, 1929.

The Big Barn. Boston: Little, Brown, 1930.

Erie Water. Boston: Little, Brown, 1933.

Mostly Canallers. Collected Stories. Boston: Little, Brown, 1934.

Drums Along the Mohawk. Boston: Little, Brown, 1936.

Chad Hanna. Boston: Little, Brown, 1940.

The Matchlock Gun. Illus. by Paul Lantz. New York: Dodd, Mead, 1941.

Tom Whipple. New York: Dodd, Mead, 1942.

Young Ames. Boston: Little, Brown, 1942.

Two Logs Crossing: John Haskell's Story. New York: Dodd, Mead, 1945.

In the Hands of the Senecas. Boston: Little, Brown, 1947.

The Wedding Journey. Boston: Little, Brown, 1947.

The First Hundred Years 1848-1948. n.p., 1948.

Wilderness Clearing. New York: Dodd, Mead, 1949.

Cadmus Henry. New York: Dodd, Mead, 1949.

Mr. Benedict's Lion. New York: Dodd, Mead, 1950.

They Fought with What They Had: The Story of the Army Air Forces in the Southwest Pacific, 1941-1942. Boston: Little, Brown, 1951.

Corporal Bess: The Story of a Boy and a Dog. New York: Dodd, Mead, 1952.

The Boyds of Black River. New York: Dodd, Mead, 1953.

Hound Dog Moses and the Promised Land. New York: Dodd, Mead, 1954.

Uncle Ben's Whale. New York: Dodd, Mead, 1955.

They Had a Horse. Illus. by Douglas Gorshine. New York: Dodd, Mead, 1962.

Three Stalwarts. Boston: Little, Brown, 1962.

The Musket and the Cross. The Struggle of France and England for North America. Boston and Toronto: Little, Brown, 1968.

Time To Go House. Illus. by Joan B. Victor. Boston and Toronto: Little, Brown, 1969.

Seven American Stories. Illus. by William Sauts Bock. Boston and Toronto: Little, Brown, 1970.

Wolf Hunt. Illus. by William Sauts Bock. Boston and Toronto: Little, Brown, 1970.

Beaver Valley. Illus. by Leslie Morrill. Boston and Toronto: Little, Brown, 1971.

The Story of Richard Storm. Illus. by William Sauts Bock. Boston and Toronto: Little, Brown, 1974.

Bert Breen's Barn. Boston and Toronto: Little, Brown, 1975.

STORIES

"'Jehu'," *Harvard Advocate* 108 (January 1, 1922): 104-108.

"The Last of the Black Dwarfs," *Harvard Advocate* 108 (March 1, 1922): 157-63.

"Black Maria," *Harvard Advocate* 108 (May 1, 1922): 231–35.

"Nosology in Extremis," *Harvard Advocate* 108 (June 20, 1922): 286–92.

"The Old 'Uns," *Harvard Advocate* 109 (November 1, 1922): 45–48.

"The Blood of His Father," *Harvard Advocate* 109 (February 1, 1923: 156–60.

"Blue Eyes." *Harvard Advocate* 110 (November 1, 1923): 47–49.

"Saint Bon and the Organist of Midnight Mass," *Harvard Advocate* 110 (January 1, 1924): 151–60.

"Julie," *Harvard Advocate* 110 (February 1924): 197–204.

"Up-River Mists and Lilacs," *Harvard Advocate* 110 (March 1, 1924): 242–45.

"The Hills," *Harvard Advocate* 110 (Class Day [June] 1924): 427–36.

"The Coming of Jan," *Harvard Advocate* 111 (September 1924): 15–19.

"A Hand Organ Out of Arcady," *Harvard Advocate* 111 (November 1924): 93–95.

"The Hanging of Kruscome Shanks," *Harvard Advocate* 111 (January 19, 1925): 191–96.

"The Devil's Angels," *Harvard Advocate* 111 (February 1925): 226–35.

"The Sacrament by the River," *Harvard Advocate* 111 (June 15, 1925): 412–21.

"The Death of Jotham Klore," *Harvard Advocate* 112 (September 1925): 21–30.

"The Second Knave," *Harvard Advocate* 112 (October 1925): 33–35.

"Solomon Tinkle's Christmas Eve," *Harvard Advocate* 112 (December, 1925), 20–28.

"The Three Wise Men," *Harvard Advocate* 112 (December 1925): 35–40. [Carried in the *Advocate* under the pseudonym of "Jean Dumaux," but reprinted, in an anthology under "Walter Edmonds."]

"The North Turret Chamber," *Harvard Advocate* 112 (February 1926): 24–36.

"The End of the Tow-Path,"*Scribner's Magazine* 80 (July 1926): 45–52.

"Who Killed Rutherford?" *Scribner's Magazine* 81 (March 1927): 303–310.

"The Voice of the Archangel," *Atlantic Monthly* 141 (January 1928): 21–41.

"My Lady's Tea," *Atlantic Monthly* 141 (March 1928): 318–25.

"The Swamper," *Dial* 84 (March 1928): 186–210.

"In the Clearing," *McCalls* 55 (May 1928): 16–17, 92.

"Duet in September," *Scribner's Magazine* 83 (June 1928): 699–709.

"Ninety," *Atlantic Monthly* 142 (August 1928): 157–70.

"Death of Red Peril: A Tragic Melodrama," *Atlantic Monthly* 142 (November 1928): 673–80.

"An Honest Deal," *Atlantic Monthly* 143 (March 1929): 300–310.

"At Schoharie Crossing," *The Forum* 81 (June 1929): 334–38, 382–84.

"The Old Jew's Tale," *The Forum* 82 (August 1929): 82–88.

"Spring Song," *Collier's* 85 (April 12, 1930): 29–30, 60, 63–64.

"The Itching Bear," *The Forum* 83 (June 1930): 344–45.

"Water Never Hurt a Man," *Harper's Magazine* 162 (December 1930): 81–86.

"Blind Eve," *Country Gentleman* 101 (July 1931): 7–8, 61–62.

"Big-Foot Sal," *Harper's Magazine* 163 (July 1931): 137–45.

"The Cruise of the Cashalot," *The Forum and Century* 87 (January 1932): 24–31.

"Heavy . . . Down," *Harper's Magazine* 165 (June 1932): 100–113.

"Black Wolf," *Saturday Evening Post* 204 (June 18, 1932): 16–17, 63, 65, 69.

"Bewitched," *Pictorial Review* 33 (September 1932): 12–13, 28–29, 38.

"Mr. Dennit's Great Adventure," *Harper's Magazine* 165 (October 1932): 560–79.

"The Trapper," *Saturday Evening Post* 205 (April 22, 1933): 10–11, 46, 49, 50, 52.

"Courtship of My Cousin Doone" (Part I), *Saturday Evening Post* 206 (October 7, 1933): 5–7, 92–96, 98, 100; (Part II), Ibid., 206 (October 14, 1933): 20–21, 97–98, 100–104, 106, 108.

"Honor of the County," *Saturday Evening Post* 206 (October 21, 1933): 8–9, 42, 44–45, 49.

"The First Race of Blue Dandy" (Part I), *Saturday Evening Post* 206 (February 24, 1934): 5–7, 48, 50–51, 53, 55; (Part II), Ibid., 206 (March 3, 1934): 26–27, 44–45, 48–51.

"Perfection of Orchard View," *Saturday Evening Post* 206 (May 19, 1934): 10–11, 63–64, 66, 70.

"Caviar to Candida," *Saturday Evening Post* 206 (June 2, 1934): 5–7, 66–67, 69–70.

"The Resurrection of Solly Moon," *Esquire* (August 1934): 47, 111, 150.

"Killers in the Valley," *Saturday Evening Post* 207 (August 4, 1934): 10–11, 34, 36–37, 39.

"The White-Nosed Colt," *Saturday Evening Post* 207 (September 8, 1934): 8–9, 72, 74–75, 77–78, 80.

"They Had a Horse," *Saturday Evening Post* 207 (March 2, 1935): 5–7, 69, 71, 74.

"Judge," *Saturday Evening Post* 208 (August 3, 1935): 10–11, 57–58, 61.

"Indian Running," *Saturday Evening Post* 208 (March 28, 1936): 5–7, 74, 76, 78.

"Escape from the Mine," *Saturday Evening Post* 208 (April 11, 1936): 10–11, 134–35, 136, 138, 140.

"Hanging Flower," *Saturday Evening Post* 208 (April 25, 1936): 22–23, 42, 44, 46, 48.

"Indians at MacKlennar's," *Saturday Evening Post* 208 (May 9, 1936): 12–13, 76, 79–80, 82, 84.

"The Captives," *Saturday Evening Post* 209 (February 13, 1937): 10–11, 35, 37–38, 40.

"Caty Breen," *Saturday Evening Post* 209 (March 20, 1937): 18–19, 85–86, 88, 90, 93–94.

"Delia Borst," *Saturday Evening Post* 209 (April 3, 1937): 14–15, 42, 45–46, 48, 50.

"Squaw," *Saturday Evening Post* 209 (April 17, 1937): 16–17, 68, 70, 73, 75, 77.

"Skanasunk," *Saturday Evening Post* 209 (May 1, 1937): 18–19, 85, 88–92.

"Dygartsbush," *Saturday Evening Post* 209 (May 15, 1937): 24–25, 76, 78, 81–84, 86–88.

"The Spanish Gun," *Saturday Evening Post* 210 (July 17, 1937): 12–13, 36, 38, 41.

"Mr. Benedict and the Madagascan Lion" (Part I), *Saturday Evening Post* 210 (February 19, 1938): 5–7, 40, 44–45, 47, 49; (Part II), Ibid., 210 (February 26, 1938): 20–21, 92–96, 98.

"Young Ames," *Saturday Evening Post* 210 (March 19, 1938): 8–9, 94–95, 97–98, 100–103.

"Arrival of the Lily Dean," *Saturday Evening Post* 210 (May 7, 1938): 5–7, 38, 40, 42, 44, 46.

"Young Ames Goes Down the River," *Saturday Evening Post* 211 (July 30, 1938): 5–7, 58–62.

"Moses," *Atlantic Monthly* 162 (August 1938): 143–52.

"Pay to the Order of John Ames," *Saturday Evening Post* 211 (November 26, 1938): 5–7, 35–36, 38, 40, 42.

"Young Ames Fights a Fire," *Saturday Evening Post* 211 (January 28, 1939): 8–9, 55–56, 60, 62.

"Tom Whipple, the Acorn, and the Emperor of Russia," *Saturday Evening Post* 211 (March 25, 1939): 5–7, 94, 96–99.

"Young Ames Makes a Deal," *Saturday Evening Post* 213 (July 13, 1940): 9–11, 84–90, 92.

"Leave It to Ames," *Saturday Evening Post* 213 (August 17, 1940): 12–13, 32, 35–36, 38.

"Young Ames, Andrew Jackson, and the American Eagle," *Saturday Evening Post* 213 (September 21, 1940): 12–13, 68, 70–72, 74.

MISCELLANEOUS PIECES (Articles, unless otherwise indicated)

"Tonight" (poem), *Harvard Advocate* 110 (January 1, 1924): 149.

"Their First Rabbit," *Forest and Stream* 94, no. 3 (March 1924): 123–24.

Review of *Boy's Own Arithmetic,* by Raymond Weeks (New York: E. P. Dutton, 1924), *Harvard Advocate* 111, no. 6 (February 1925): 242–44.

"Beginners Both. A Beagle's First Winter in the Field," *Forest and Stream* 95, no. 3 (March 1925): 150–51, 184–86.

Review of *Jungle-Born,* by John Eyton (New York: Century Company, 1925), *Harvard Advocate* 111, no. 10 (June 15, 1925): 433.

"The Hind-Quarters of an Elephant," *Harvard Advocate* 112 (September 1925): 35–37.

Review of *Drums,* by James Boyd (New York: Scribner's, 1925), *Harvard Advocate* 112, no. 1 (September, 1925): 60–62.

"The Gum-Didderators of Football," *Harvard Advocate* 112 (October 1925): 17–20.

Review of *The Rector of Maliseet,* by Leslie Reed (New York: E. P. Dutton, 1925), *Harvard Advocate* 112, no. 2 (October 1925): 60–61.

"The Abbot Speaks" (poem), *Harvard Advocate* 112 (November 1925): 25–26.

"The Coast Farmer" (poem), *Harvard Advocate* 112 (January 1926): 20.

"The Platonic Fisherman," *Harvard Advocate* 112 (May 1926): 25–28.

Review of *Starbrace,* by Sheila Kaye-Smith (New York: E. P. Dutton, 1926), *Harvard Advocate* 112, no. 9 (May, 1926): 44–45.

Autobiographical sketch in *Authors Today and Yesterday,* ed. Stanley J. Kunitz. (New York: H. W. Wilson, 1933): 221–22.

"Upstate," *Atlantic Monthly* 156 (November 1935): 591–99.

"How You Begin a Novel," *Atlantic Monthly* 158 (August 1936): 189–92.

"Introduction." In *Rome Haul* (New York: Modern Library, 1938), pp. vii–xii.

"My Friends, the Collaborators," *Harvard Alumni Bulletin* 42, no. 27 (May 3, 1940): 932–34.

"A Novelist Takes Stock," *Atlantic Monthly* 172 (July 1943): 73–77.

Review of *Canal Town,* by Samuel Hopkins Adams (New York: Random House, 1944), *Atlantic Monthly* 73 (June 1944): 125.

"Author's Note." In Bertha Mahoney Miller and Elinor Whitney Field, eds. *Newbery Medal Books; 1922-1955,* Horn Book Papers, 1 (Boston: The Horn Book, 1955): pp. 210-11.

"Jack Darby on Writing Books for Children" (Acceptance Paper). In Bertha Mahoney Miller and Elinor Whitney Field, eds. *Newbery Medal Books: 1922-1955.* Horn Book Papers, 1 (Boston: The Horn Book, 1955): 212-24.

"The Erie Canal. The Story of the Digging of Clinton's Ditch" (booklet) (Utica, N.Y.: Munson-Williams-Proctor Institute, 1960).

Index

WALTER D. EDMONDS, Storyteller

was composed in 10-point Compugraphic Century Schoolbook and leaded two points,
with display type in Century Schoolbook by Metricomp Studio,
and photoreproduced Cloister Cursive initials by J. M. Bundscho, Inc.;
printed on 55-pound, acid-free Glatfelter Antique Cream paper stock,
Smythe-sewn and bound over boards in Joanna Arrestox B,
by Maple-Vail Book Manufacturing Group, Inc.;
and published by

SYRACUSE UNIVERSITY PRESS
Syracuse, New York 13210